# *ADVANCED WRITING HANDBOOK*

## *for*

## *ESOL*

**Fourth Edition**

**John Sparks**
*Portland Community College*

**KENDALL/HUNT PUBLISHING COMPANY**
4050 Westmark Drive    Dubuque, Iowa 52002

# TABLE OF CONTENTS

## THE COLLEGE WRITING PAPER

# PREFACE

This handbook is designed for ESOL students in their final quarter of an ESOL academic writing sequence. The *Advanced Writing Handbook for ESOL* grew out of *The ENNL Handbook for the Research Paper* and the materials prepared by ESOL instructors at Portland Community College for writing assignments at the highest level of writing in the ESOL program.

I would like to thank Janet Leamy, Kate Carney, Laura Horani, Elise McLain, Roxanne Hill, Christina Sparks, Ilka Kuznik, and Ali Modabber for their suggestions and handouts contributed to the handbook. I am of course grateful to those students from our classes, as well as those who had work published in *The Ambassador*, the magazine of ESOL student writing at Portland Community College, whose assignments are used as examples.

A special mention must be reserved for Jean Ady, who co-authored the first three editions of this handbook. Jean's work on those editions was an essential foundation for this edition. In addition, I would like to thank the following for giving permission to reprint materials in the Handbook: Nicholas Kristof of *The New York Times* and Albert Shanker of *On Campus*.

John Sparks
ESOL Instructor
Sylvania Campus
P.C.C.

Fourth edition,
November 2007

# To the Instructor: Suggestions for Using the Handbook

This handbook is not exhaustive and, indeed, has been kept to a certain length to reduce the costs for students. Instructors should provide supplementary materials as needed. In addition, the handbook is not intended to be used in sequence. Instructors should cover the section on **Preparation** as they are working through the **Rhetorical Styles** section. We encourage instructors to come up with their own prewriting tasks relating specifically to the topic they have chosen for the assignment.

The research paper section of the handbook seems lengthy considering the fact that, in many classes, only one research paper will be written. It is not intended that the students memorize documentation conventions: the handbook is designed to serve as a reference. Indeed, it should prove useful to students in the years after they leave an ESOL program. Students should be cautioned, however, that different disciplines and different instructors advocate conventions other than the M.L.A. style we follow here.

# THE COLLEGE WRITING PAPER

## PREPARATION

### Selecting a Topic

When selecting a topic for a paper, it is important to **narrow** the subject. A large, very general subject, for example "My City," cannot be dealt with in very much detail in a short paper of two to four typed pages. Therefore, it is necessary to narrow your topic so that you can supply as many interesting details as possible and treat the subject **in depth**.

Example: Let's take the topic "My City" and see how it can be narrowed.

| | |
|---|---|
| Step 1: general subject | My City: Mexico City |
| Step 2: more specific subject | Mexico City: the Zócalo |
| Step 3: even more specific subject | The Zócalo: sunset |
| Step 4: | The Zócalo: sunset, summer |
| Step 5: | The Zócalo: sunset, summer; lowering the national flag |
| Step 6: | The Zócalo: sunset, summer; lowering the national flag; watching from the steps of the Cathedral |

By going through a step-by-step approach to narrowing the topic, you can find a suitable subject for a short paper. Notice that the final topic (Step 6) gives you a very specific focus for a description essay in terms of place: " Zócalo"; time: "sunset"; season: "summer"; and perspective: "from the steps of the Cathedral."

In addition, while selecting a topic, you need to be acutely aware of your **audience**. For the immediate purpose of your college writing, the audience consists of your peers (classmates) and your instructor. However, always also think in terms of a broader audience of readers so that you can focus on making your writing clear, interesting, and useful. Understand that some topics may need some detailed explanation because your audience may not know much about them. Conversely, avoid wasting words and space on topics that are already well-known and obvious to your readers.

## Exercise 1

Try to narrow the following topic in six steps. This is not an outline: it is a method of narrowing the topic.

Step 1:    A problem with technology

Step 2:

Step 3:

Step 4:

Step 5:

Step 6:

## Exercise 2

Now use this step by step system to get a narrow topic for your first essay:

Step 1:

Step 2:

Step 3:

Step 4:

Step 5:

Step 6:

# Outlining

When you have done all your thinking and perhaps some reading for the paper, it is time to make a brief outline. This outline should reflect all the topical divisions of the paper, as well as the paper's organization.

Below is a sample paper outline.

---

**Topic: Computer viruses**

I.     Introduction:
       "hook" (an anecdote)
       computer viruses: the problems
       thesis statement

II.    Solutions:

     A.     buy an antivirus program
     B.     install a firewall
     C.     install all updates
     D.     scan your e-mail
     E.     use correct web addresses

III.   Conclusion:
       summary of main points


Source:     Guillaume D'Amico, "Infect Me If You Can!"

---

We can see from the outline that this essay will consist of seven paragraphs: I, IIA, IIB, IIC, IID, IIE, III.

## Sample Essay Outline

Title: _____

**First paragraph (Introduction):**    Think of an interesting anecdote, quote, example, etc., to begin. Write the **thesis statement**.

_____

_____

**First body paragraph:** Topic sentence + details and examples

_____

_____

_____

**Next paragraph:** Topic sentence + details and examples

_____

_____

_____

**Next paragraph:** Topic sentence + details and examples

_____

_____

_____

**Final paragraph: (Conclusion):**    Give a summarizing statement, opinion, prediction, or solution.

_____

_____

**PLEASE NOTE: A good essay at this level could have as few as four paragraphs or as many as seven, eight, nine, or more! You do not have to try and fit all your ideas into a five-paragraph outline.**

# The Thesis Statement

Now that you have a good idea of what you are going to write about, you need to write a **thesis statement**. The thesis statement is usually the final sentence in the introductory paragraph. It declares the author's purpose in writing the paper.

A thesis statement can be defined as <u>an opinion which can be defended</u>. It should tell the reader the <u>main idea</u> of the paper. It is <u>not</u> a question, but a clear statement of opinion which can be supported by the body of your essay. It should:

1. consist of a single grammatical sentence;
2. mention your specific topic;
3. (optional) contain the aspects of your topic
   (e.g. specific solutions to a problem);
4. reveal your <u>purpose</u>;
5. must show that the topic is <u>controversial</u> and <u>open for debate</u>,
   i.e. there may be many opinions other than your own;
6. be the <u>final sentence</u> of your introductory paragraph.

Remember that you should select a thesis (topic and purpose) which will be <u>interesting</u>, <u>informative</u>, and <u>thought-provoking</u> for your teacher and your classmates. A thesis statement also usually needs to be connected to the rest of the introductory paragraph by a **transition sentence**. You will be supporting your thesis in later paragraphs with facts, statistics, anecdotes, examples, and other relevant details.

<u>What is **NOT** a good thesis statement (or topic)</u>

At this level of writing, please refrain from choosing a topic which is already very well-known to your audience, or which may be too obvious, or uninteresting, for example:

"There are three kinds of shows that people watch on T.V.: dramas, sit-coms, and the nightly news."

"Drinking alcohol may cause traffic accidents, family problems, and health problems."

"Los Angeles and New York are very different cities"

In addition, avoid <u>vague</u> or general thesis statements, for example:

**NOT:**     "School uniforms have many advantages."

**BUT:**     "Those who support school uniforms say that they help to decrease discipline problems and instill a sense of school spirit."

At this level of writing, a thesis statement should **NOT** represent one of the following:

a) a well-known fact

"The United States has four seasons: winter, spring, summer, and fall." (Everyone in your audience knows this.)

b) a belief

"Rap music comes from the devil." (You cannot <u>prove</u> this point in an essay or convince others who don't have the same beliefs as you do).

c) a question

"Should teachers give students grades?" (Your thesis should be a <u>statement</u> of your opinion on a subject).

d) a personal expression of intent (in expository essays)

"Now I am going to tell you about the problem of smoking." (In expository writing, you need to leave out the word 'I' and be more objective).

e) a blanket statement

"Children in America watch too much T.V." (Use modals such as 'may' or 'might' and qualifying adjectives such as 'many' or some').

# The Good Thesis Statement

## The thesis statement should not be too <u>broad</u>.

Reason:       The topic will be too large to cover in a brief essay. Your topic (and thesis) should be narrow enough so that you can write about it in detail.

**Too broad:**    Southern California is a beautiful place to take a vacation.
**Narrowed:**    San Diego has many attractions that beckon to visitors from around the world.
**Narrowed further:**    The splendid beach at Coronado is a perfect spot to while away a few hours or days of vacation.

**Too broad:**    There are many kinds of office workers.
**Narrowed:**    The workers on the line at the IMS Meatpacking Plant range from dedicated and professional to slow and unreliable.

**Too broad:**    Congress should create more wilderness areas.
**Narrowed:**    The U.S. Congress should designate another 3 million acres of wilderness in National Forest lands in the western states.

## The thesis statement should be <u>committed</u>.

Reason:       You need to focus on a clear point. If you are uncommitted, your essay will "drift" from one point to another without any focus. A good thesis statement should clearly indicate the writer's opinion (but don't use phrases like "in my opinion" or "I think."

**Uncommitted:**    People disagree about whether talking on cell phones should be allowed while driving.
**Committed:**    There should be a law against using a cell phone while driving because the practice is demonstrably dangerous.

**Uncommitted:**    The Statue of Liberty is one of the places to visit in New York City.
**Committed:**    The Statue of Liberty is one of the prime attractions of New York City because of its history, interesting construction, and wonderful views.

**Uncommitted:**    Smoking in bars can be harmful to the health of people who work there.
**Committed:**    There should be a state law against smoking in bars and nightclubs because the people who work there are likely to suffer serious health problems from second-hand smoke.

**The thesis statement should be <u>clear</u>.**

Reason:    A thesis statement that is unclear may be badly written or may not get to the point. An unclear thesis statement should be completely rewritten to begin with the topic of the essay.

**Unclear:**    Elderly people need to exercise.
**Clear:**      Elderly people will experience a rapid decline in physical ability unless they regularly do light exercise, such as walking, swimming, or weight-training.

**Unclear:**    There are a lot of unfortunate issues caused by people who immigrate to my country illegally.
**Clear:**      A rising crime rate, the straining of government services, and increasing discrimination are all the result of higher numbers of illegal immigrants in Ghana.

**Unclear:**    The Estonian term *tubli* means "hard-working" and many other things.
**Clear:**      The Estonian word *tubli*, meaning hard-working, honest, productive, and helpful to others, can be used for parents, students, and workers alike.


**The thesis statement should not be <u>a fact</u>.**

Reason:    A thesis statement is based on an opinion, as is your entire essay. Otherwise, you are simply writing a report and not an essay.

**Fact:**       Alaska can be divided into six main geographical regions: the Arctic, West Coast, Interior, South Central, Western Maritime, and Eastern Maritime.
**Opinion:**    Alaska's Interior region offers the most remote and compelling destinations for the seasoned outdoor adventurer.

**Fact:**       In 1988, the State of Florida declared that English was its official language.
**Opinion:**    Florida's English-only law should be repealed because the state's non-English-speaking residents now have even greater difficulty accessing government services.

**Fact:**       Many people disagree about sending humans to Mars.
**Opinion:**    The United States should cease funding the planned manned expedition to Mars because there are more pressing and useful projects in space on which we can spend our dollars.

Examples of thesis statements

**Description:** *
"When I was a young boy, I especially enjoyed the times that my uncle Woo took me fishing on the South China Sea."

"The highlight of my first art exhibition was the period before the opening ceremony."

**Classification:**
"Book lovers can be categorized into three major groups according to the way they treat their books."

"Many teachers show favoritism, but they show favoritism in different ways."

**Cause/Effect:**
"In Iran, divorce is usually the result of money problems, lack of empowerment or hasty commitment."

"The relatively new trolley bus system in Quito, Ecuador, has brought many beneficial effects to the city."

**Problem/Solution:**
"The theft of stereos from cars is a serious problem in San Francisco; however, there are several ways to control the situation."

"If you have SAD (seasonal affective disorder), you have to take the appropriate treatment to survive the season.

**Definition:**
"Ambition has both positive and negative qualities depending on how a person tries to reach his or her goals."

"A good mother should be a good example, teacher and friend for her children, and she should also devote herself to them."

**Argument:**
"The U.S. should consider instituting a same-sex public school system because this would allow students to study without being distracted by the opposite sex."

"Parents should avoid spanking their children because it is neither necessary nor appropriate and can actually increase the child's defiant behavior."

---

\* Descriptive essays do not need an obvious thesis statement. However, the thesis (topic and controlling idea) should be clear to the reader.

Exercise 3

Try to think of a suitable thesis statement for the following topics.

1.   **Eating at fast-food restaurants**

2.   **Different kinds of computer users**

3.   **What is a good father?**

4.   **Walking dogs without a leash**

5.   **Your favorite place on the ocean**

6.   **What is honesty?**

7.   **Grading practices at college**

8.   **The reasons for the high cost of textbooks**

9.   **Different ways that people eat rice**

10.   **Keeping a balanced life as a full-time student with a job**

# The Introduction

An introductory paragraph in an essay usually comes in two parts: first, the attention-getting ideas, or "hook", which introduce the topic to the reader; these are followed by the **thesis statement**. Often, you will need a **transition sentence** between the first part of your introduction and the thesis statement.

Writing a good introduction to an essay takes skill and careful thought. It is important to write a paragraph that will convince the reader that the essay is worth reading. YOUR TITLE IS **NOT** YOUR INTRODUCTION. Some effective ways to introduce an essay are to:

1. write about an interesting incident/issue in the news related to the topic;
2. use an anecdote (a short narrative concerning a particular incident);
3. identify yourself as an expert on the topic;
4. use facts and statistics about the topic;
5. use an appropriate quotation;
6. write a vivid description;
7. discuss a shared experience;
8. ask a rhetorical question.

The introduction should not seem 'tacked-on': it must be an <u>integral</u> part of your essay. The <u>length</u> of your introduction must not seem out of proportion with the rest of your essay.

**Poor introductions (first sentences of an essay)**

1. The very general, very shallow statement:

   "Food is a very important thing in human life."

2. The made-up conversation:

   "Recently, I was chatting with my high school friends about how to classify teachers in terms of their classroom methodology."

3. A leap right into the topic:

   "Eating and drinking should be permitted in college classes."

   (This would be all right for a <u>thesis statement</u>, but is <u>not</u> a good first sentence)

4. The personal question:

   "What do you think about a law against using a cell phone while driving?"

5. Using the word "I":

   "I think that people should not have more than one child."

## A bad introduction

Everywhere in the world, people live in houses. However, some people are homeless. Homeless people don't live in houses. They live on the streets. There are some homeless people in my country. I have seen some homeless people when I walk in my city. Homeless people need to find a bathroom and they need to find a place to sleep. Sometimes they get sick. People are homeless for many reasons.

Problems:

1. Very vague, general or obvious opening sentences.
2. Language is simple; sentences are very short.
3. Paragraph is general, with one specific sentence: "There are some homeless people in my country," then becomes general again.
4. Writer is vague about places: "my country."
5. No good transition from introduction to thesis statement (moves directly from effects to causes.
6. Thesis statement is not specific: "many reasons."

## A good introduction

I remember a homeless man whom I saw almost every morning on the way to school in my hometown of Fukuoka, in southern Japan. Crossing through a narrow park in a valley surrounded by high-rise apartments, I would see a man who wore a dusty, old-fashioned business jacket and a very large pair of pants full of holes. He had long, gray hair and a beard, and his gloomy eyes were like those of a dead fish. In the park, he read books almost every day, sitting up straight on a bench. He was one of the educated 'furousha', or homeless people, whose number is estimated to be 100,000 in Japan. The furousha have become homeless because of their inability to cope with modern, fast-paced society.

**Yukiko Higuma**

Strengths:

1. Begins with an interesting anecdote which has many excellent details.
2. Language is sophisticated, with a variety of sentence structures.
3. Paragraph is specific, with anecdotal and factual evidence.
4. Writer is specific about places: "Fukuoka, Japan" and uses specific terminology: "furousha."
5. Excellent transition from anecdote to facts to thesis statement.
6. Thesis statement is specific and clear.

## More examples of introductory paragraphs

Here are some examples of the eight types of introductory paragraphs from student papers. The <u>thesis statement</u> is underlined. Note that most of these paragraphs also have a <u>transition sentence</u> which connects the first part of the introduction to the thesis statement.

### 1. Write about an interesting incident/issue in the news related to the topic

A recent study made in Boston found that many young people are starting their own businesses. They are doing this more than older people, who more often work for companies or the government. The article entitled "Young and Going It Alone," which appeared in newspaper, shows there is success for many young people every year in the United States. According to the article, more young people than ever before want to work for themselves. They don't want other people controlling them on their jobs. <u>Opening one's own business is one of many options for young Americans, but it is the only option available for many young Vietnamese</u>.

**Phuc Ma**

### 2. Use an anecdote (a short narrative concerning a particular incident)

It happened eight years ago back home in Colombia. All the members of my family and our close friends had a big party over at my Uncle Jorge's country home. It was around 5:00 p.m., and all of the guests had arrived, but my uncle was still in a neighboring town executing some business. We were waiting for him the whole night, but he never showed up. A week passed, and we hadn't heard a word from him or about him. Then my family got an anonymous letter from an organized crime group. It said we had 15 days to pay them an outlandish amount of money; otherwise, he would be killed. Unfortunately, this situation is not unique in my country. As can be confirmed through different mass media communication, kidnapping is one of the most common social problems burdening my country. <u>Kidnapping in Colombia will end only when families refuse to negotiate with criminals</u>.

**Maria Carolina Afanador**

### 3. Identify yourself as an expert on the topic

Bamboo has been my all time favorite plant since I was a little girl. It contributed to my happy childhood: fishing with my father on hot summer days by the river, lying on the grass and feeling the wind blow, watching bamboo trees swaying, listening to their sounds. These are memories that will never fade. Recently I was fascinated by the beauty of the thick bamboo forest in Ang Lee's movie *Crouching Tiger, Hidden Dragon*, as I watched the dreamy scene of two characters clinging to the tops of swaying bamboo trees and waging a deadly sword fight. I began cultivating bamboo ten years ago. In that time I've grown to appreciate its special qualities. <u>Bamboo is simultaneously hard and soft, its stems and straight but flexible, and its leaves are graceful and green all year around</u>.

**Kiki Gavin**

## 4. Use facts and statistics about the topic

The World Bank, one of the strongest international financial organizations, was formed in 1944. At present, over 180 countries, which are represented by governors, have joined the World Bank as member nations. The seven richest nations-- Canada, France, Germany, Italy, Japan, the United Kingdom, and the United States--have 44 percent of the voting power in the organization. Moreover, the United States, which is the largest shareholder, has the power to forbid any changes in the World Bank's capital base and the Articles of Agreement. The main goals of the World Bank are to promote sustainable economic development and to reduce poverty throughout the world by providing loans, guarantees, and related technical assistance for projects and programs in its developing member countries. In spite of its high-minded goals, the World Bank is considered a failure by many of the world's economists. Unfortunately, the track record of the World Bank is far from successful in giving a helping hand to developing countries.

**Mathew Chu**

## 5. Use an appropriate quotation

Imagination is a quality that all human beings possess. That doesn't mean, however, that everyone uses it in the same manner. Some people use imagination for very cruel purposes, letting all kinds of negative thoughts fill their minds or flying completely away from reality. I like to use my imagination to dream while I'm awake in order to visualize a better future. One of my favorite quotations comes from the scientist Carl Sagan, who said: " Imagination will often carry us to worlds that never were. But without it, we go nowhere." This idea has given me comfort many times as I struggle to make a new life for myself and my family here in the United States.

**Mileth Vidales**

## 6. Write a vivid description

Brazil—where unemployment, social inequality, poverty, and corruption are always issues—finds its relief in the Carnival. In Portuguese spelled "Carnaval," it is known by Brazilian people as a time to party. When I was growing up, the warm summer season was always a reminder of Christmas, New Year's, and Carnaval. During Carnaval, foolish behavior is expected. Kids throw eggs and water balloons at each other, and there is lively music everywhere. Television channels focus their cameras on unclothed people who let go of their inhibitions completely. Some dress in costumes, and some don't, but they all dance and drink. Today's Carnaval is a reflection of ancient festivals in Europe. Blending all social levels, Carnaval is not only a wild time that has no boundaries but also a kind of illusion that covers an unwanted reality.

**Artur Aoko**

## 7. Discuss a shared experience

To many students, writing in English is often boring, demanding, and time consuming. They sometimes feel that writing takes too much time away from working on other homework or activities like playing games on the computer or enjoying time with friends and loved ones. This is not true though for students who view writing as an ideal learning tool for the process of learning English and meeting challenges in school or the workplace. What makes writing so special to me? Writing is essential to my life and is a tool that will help me succeed. <u>Writing is enjoyable, therapeutic, educational, and relaxing.</u>

**Tupu Soliga**

## 8. Ask a rhetorical question

What is the greatest challenge for a parent who is struggling to be successful in college? When I accepted the challenge to start back to school last year, I thought that returning to college would make me a better person; instead, I turned into a monster. While I was trying to make an effort to improve my own skills, I was failing to be an effective mother. I was so wrapped up in my studies that I forgot to prioritize my role as a parent. My priorities shifted, and I did not realize how badly this was affecting my daughter. Consequently, she was turning into a little rascal, and I was about to lose my mind. The environment at home was very tense, and at the end of the day, both my daughter and I were upset, anxious, and unhappy. After two terms, I finally realized that my relationship with my daughter had become estranged. <u>When I figured out how to solve my problem, I came to know and accept myself in a new way.</u>

**May Donohue**

# The Body Paragraphs

The body paragraphs are the longest section of your essay. They should make up at least 75 percent of the total length of your paper. Each paragraph should contain one **main idea** and should be developed with such details as statistics, facts, anecdotes, examples, stories of personal experience, descriptive details and explanations.

Each body paragraph usually contains a **topic sentence**, which is often the first sentence in the paragraph. Topic sentences sometimes begin with a transition word or phrase, such as 'On the other hand', 'As a result', 'First', 'Second', 'Finally', 'A different . . .', 'Another . . .' Transition words may also be used to connect ideas within a paragraph.

Body paragraphs move from **general** to **specific** information. After the topic sentence, there may be a brief explanation, but then the paragraph should be developed using interesting details. A body paragraph should be several sentences in length. One or two sentences does not make a paragraph. Remember that all the information in each of the body paragraphs must relate directly to your **thesis**.

Be careful with **verb tenses** when writing paragraphs. General information that shows facts that are always true should be expressed using the **present simple** tense. Examples of past events in your own life or historical events should be expressed using the **past simple** tense.

Here are some examples of body paragraphs; the topic sentence is underlined.

### Topic: Problems with Wikipedia

Many skeptics claim that Wikipedia relies too much on anonymous internet users to edit articles. However, this fits Wikipedia's principle of having users write and correct information, showing that "collaboration can create good work" (O'Leary). According to Wikipedia, shared knowledge covers topics more broadly. By giving people the opportunity to edit information, there are fewer chances to have misleading or wrong information because the articles are continually reviewed and kept up-to-date by users. The skeptics state that this freedom can compromise some of the information in Wikipedia. *The New York Times* revealed that Essjay, a volunteer who edited information for many articles in Wikipedia, was really a 24-year-old with no PhD in Theology or degree in Canon Law as he had stated (Maich). This highlights one of Wikipedia's main weaknesses: users have to trust information, which may be edited by people who misrepresent their educational background and qualifications.

**Javier Trinidad-Sanchez**

**Topic: Work schedules of doctors in residency**

Eugene F Barasch, M. D., PhD., believes that part of a physician's training is to learn how to work effectively while tired ( "Mandate Time Off"). On the contrary, studies from Harvard University show that "working for 24 hours is hazardous" (Fakelman). When a person has been without sleep for more that eighteen hours, he or she can zone out. Other studies made by the American Medical Association in 2005 indicate that staying awake for 24 hours is equal to having a blood alcohol level of .10. The question is, would you like to be helped by a drunk doctor? What about getting surgery from the same sleepy, intoxicated mind? Or perhaps why not one of your relatives or a friend?

**Magdalena Valdivieso**

**Topic: Great feelings from great paintings**

American folk-art paintings, such as some painted by Charles Wysocki or Mattie Lou O'Kelley, always make me feel happy when I look at them. There are always houses, trees, flowers, farms, happy folks - many beautiful things in the pictures. I learn about the changes in the land and the different seasons. Everyone is living together in harmony. Men are working on the farm or making handicrafts. Women are sitting together, making many different kinds of fruit pies in the kitchen: apple pies, cherry pies, pumpkin pies, berry pies - they look delicious! On holidays, everyone gathers around in a very big house and has a party. Some people are dancing or looking after their babies. Children are playing and running around the house. Some also try to steal food from the kitchen when everyone is busy. When I look at these paintings, I can feel their happiness. It is just like listening to some soft music. I wish I were living in their world.

**Kwong Ngai Hung**

**Topic: Marijuana for medicinal purposes**

One of marijuana's therapeutic benefits is its ability to suppress the nausea and vomiting suffered by many patients undergoing anti-cancer chemotherapy. Conventional antiemetic medications often fail to control these symptoms, and the main active substance in marijuana, delta-9tetrahydrocannibol (THC) taken orally appeared to be less effective than crude marijuana. Marijuana's vapour is easily absorbed and acts quickly. Moreover, other cannabinoids in the marijuana plant may modify the action of THC (Grinspoon 1876). Users can fine-tune the dose for themselves. Having marijuana cigarettes under their control allows chemotherapy patients to ease their feelings of helplessness ("Marijuana as a Medicine" ). In a 1990 poll, more than 40% of American oncologists revealed they had suggested that patients smoke marijuana for the relief of nausea induced by chemotherapy ("Cannabis and Medicine").

**Margarita Vainiene**

## Coherence in body paragraphs

A body paragraph needs to hold together as a unit, i.e. it needs to have **coherence**. There are several ways to maintain coherence in a body paragraph:

1. Refer to old information when introducing new information, for example:

> *Few students understand the importance of seeing a college advisor early in their years at college. <u>Students who do not see a college advisor</u> may waste time and money taking courses they do not need. Indeed, my friend Artur <u>was such a student</u>. He . . . . .*

2. Use words which are related to each other in the given context:

> *<u>Phishers</u> use <u>electronic communication</u>, such as <u>e-mail</u> and <u>instant messaging</u>, to gain <u>sensitive information</u> that they can use <u>for criminal purposes</u>. Such information may include <u>passwords</u> or <u>account numbers</u>. <u>PayPal users</u> have been targeted in the . . . .*

3. Use parallel structures:

> *Victims of abuse need to articulate clearly <u>when the incident happened</u> and <u>what exactly occurred</u>. They need to <u>maintain consistency</u>, <u>focus on the facts</u>, and <u>remember details</u>. It is only when . . . . . .*

4. Use demonstrative pronouns (*this, that, these, those*) and lots of examples:

> *The clearing below the waterfall was bathed in filtered sunlight. <u>This</u> induced a sense of other-worldliness which made us feel like privileged visitors. Shafts of sunlight seemed to select individual <u>rocks, twigs, leaves, flowers, and pools</u> for display. <u>These</u> glowed in the half-light like . . . . . .*

5. Use linking words, such as coordinating and subordinating conjunctions and transition words:

> *There are designated smoking areas on campus, <u>but</u> they are often ignored by smokers. <u>Therefore</u>, campus authorities need to <u>either</u> enforce use of these areas <u>or</u> consider an outright ban on smoking. <u>Unless</u> enforcement is effective, anti-smoking advocates are likely to push for a ban <u>and</u> . . . . . . .*

> Note: Please restrain yourself in the use of transition words. Often better connections are made with coordinating and subordinating conjunctions. A paragraph heavy with transition words does not a good paragraph make.

Exercise 4

1. Write a short paragraph of four sentences or more that begins with the sentence below. Refer to information in the previous sentence as you write a new sentence.

*Some managers are very good at telling people what to do, but they often do not perform very well themselves.*

2. Write a short paragraph of four sentences or more that begins with the sentence below. Use related words and terms to build context.

*A good teacher also builds an atmosphere of trust and comfort in the classroom.*

3. Write a short paragraph of four sentences or more that begins with the sentence below. Use two or three parallel structures.

*Not everybody loves dogs, and dog owners need to recognize this fact when they take their pets outside the home.*

4. Write a short paragraph of four sentences or more that begins with the sentence below. Use demonstrative pronouns and examples.

*The college needs to furnish its classrooms with more comfortable chairs.*

5. Write a short paragraph of four sentences or more that begins with the sentence below. Use transition words and conjunctions to connect ideas.

*Panhandling discourages downtown shoppers and adversely affects business in the area.*

## Topic Sentences

Use topic sentences for the body paragraphs of your essays. Topic sentences are more general sentences which tell the reader the main idea of the paragraph. A topic sentence is often the first sentence in the paragraph. Sometimes, it might be the second sentence if the first sentence is transitional. A topic sentence may also appear later in the paragraph.

### Exercise 5

Write appropriate topic sentences for the following paragraphs taken from student essays:

1. _____

_____ . We had a swing for a baby, and we decided to use it. Daniel has been able to sit in the swing since his first month, so we had him sit in it and made him swing when he was crying, and we could see our beautiful baby falling asleep. Oh, thank God! Finally, my husband and I had a peaceful night with our baby thanks to the swing. However, that method has an important rule: you have to watch the baby while he is sleeping in a swing and move him to his crib if you want to go to bed. If we do not do so, it is not safe for a baby. Therefore, we moved him and were very careful not to wake him, and then we slept.

**Chunhee Yim**

2. _____

_____ . They said that they would not allow their children to watch violent cartoons. When asked about those programs, one of them said: "As the mother of three boys, I have seen how these programs affect not only how they play with other children, but how they view the world. These shows teach children how to solve problems with violence." Another parent complained: "My child has watched cartoon shows such as *G.I. Joe* and *The Master of the Universe*, and his behavior is markedly more aggressive and violent after viewing these shows."

**Buoi Vo**

3. _____

_____ . Chinese people have a saying: "Like father, like son." Because mothers usually spend more time with their children than fathers, the mother's behavior is the family's most important influence on the kids. I have a friend who told me the story of a woman named Shelly. She had a daughter when she was sixteen years old, and she didn't even know who the father of her daughter was. She not only drank and smoked but also had numerous sexual relationships. Her daughter turned out exactly the same way as she did. She had a baby boy when she was a teenager. Now Shelly is a 31-year-old grandmother.

**Della Muse**

4.  _____

_____ . The field was only three hundred square meters. There was a ditch beside the field, and I could hear the murmuring of a stream. The sky looked like cotton candy. The field was completely covered with colorful ripe vegetables: bright red tomatoes, fresh dark green cucumbers, and purplish eggplants. The heavy-looking vegetables almost reached the ground, as though they made a polite bow from the waist. They basked under a burning sun like jewels. The dried out soil of my grandmother's field gave the surface of the ground the appearance of the being covered with powdered sugar.

**Manami Omori**

Exercise 6

Fill in the following paragraphs with your own ideas and examples. Each paragraph begins with a topic sentence.

1.  There are several simple steps that I follow in order to make my English as

clear as possible to native speakers. The first step is _____

_____

_____

For example, _____

_____

_____

_____

2.  Cell phones can be useful in many ways. One benefit of cell phones is _____

_____

_____ . For instance, _____

_____

_____

Another benefit is _____

_____ . An example of this is _____

_____

3.　　One kind of supervisor is _____

_____ . This kind of supervisor _____

_____

_____

For example, _____

_____

_____

_____

## Exercise 7

Choose <u>two</u> of the following topic sentences and, on a separate sheet of paper, write short paragraphs, with appropriate details and examples, to support them.

1.　　Video games may be one reason for increased violence in school playgrounds.

2.　　Suddenly, we heard a slight noise from the bushes ahead of us.

3.　　Requiring uniforms in public schools would ensure that students from wealthy families would not look any different from students from poor families.

4.　　Some people simply enjoy meaningless and endless conversations on the phone.

5.　　Parents should ask themselves the question: "Are we doing damage to our children by putting them into day care during the first year of their lives?"

6.　　Another way to deal with a problem neighbor is to find someone who will act as a mediator.

# The Conclusion

The concluding paragraph of your essay is an integral part of the paper, just like the introduction. Your conclusion should be <u>brief</u> and should also relate directly to your **thesis**. A conclusion should **NOT** introduce a new aspect of the topic or a new example. A good conclusion may involve:

1. a prediction (what may happen in the future);
2. a suggestion, piece of advice, or recommendation;
3. a proposed solution (briefly) to the issue discussed in your paper;
4. a comparison (briefly) to a new or different situation;
5. a restatement of your thesis or opinion (in different words);
6. a summary of the main points derived from your essay.


<u>Exercise 8</u>

Look at the examples of student essays in the next section of this textbook and discuss how each writer concluded his or her essay based on the methods listed above.


1.     "An Unforgettable Trip"  p. 37

2.     "My Last Climb"  p. 38

3.     "Many Ways to Turn a Page"  p. 45

4.     "First Families"  p. 47

5.     *"Ishindenshin"*  p. 55

6.     "A Good Husband"  p. 56

7.     "An Incomplete Education"  p. 63

8.     "Domestic Terror Strikes Hard"  p. 64

9.     "Don't Be a Target"  p. 71

10.     "Sense of Place"  p. 73

11.     "Save the Planet"  p. 85

12.     "Keep Your Hands to Yourself!"  p. 87

# The Title

It is harder than you think to make a good title for your essay. A title should be **short**: it is **not a full sentence** and may omit some some function words, such as articles, helping verbs, verb 'to be', or pronouns. Good titles do not necessarily define your exact topic. Rather, they will use an **intriguing** or **'catchy'** phrase to make the reader want to read the essay. Titles often pose a question that the reader will want to see answered in the essay.

Examples of 'catchy' titles

a.	for an essay about students who study hard in high school:

**"Why Don't We Just 'Goof Off'?"**

b.	for an essay about the kinds of people who eat popcorn at movie theaters:

**"Salt and Butter, Please"**

Sometimes titles can come in two parts, a 'catchy' phrase followed by a **colon** and a topic statement, for example:

c.	for an essay about the reasons for poor eating habits:

**"Junk Diets: Why We Eat Trash"**

d.	for an essay about the problem of dogs that bark all night:

**"Muzzle Your Mutt: Taking Care of a Neighborhood Nuisance."**

Try to make your title <u>interesting</u>. It should catch the reader's eye and make them want to read further.

Examples of poor titles

a.	Don't make the kind of essay you are writing into a title, e.g.:

**"Problem/Solution Essay"**

b.	Don't make the title of your essay too obvious, e.g.:

**"The Reasons Why Students Drop Out of College"**

c.	Don't make your title into a complete sentence, e.g.

**"Doctor-assisted Suicide Should Be Against the Law"**

Remember that your title should be **centered on the page** and should be in the same **plain, 12-point font** as the rest of your essay. All words in the title should be capitalized except for articles, conjunctions, and prepositions of two and three letters.

Exercise 9

Think of some good titles for the following topics:

1.    A descriptive essay about a favorite picnic spot.

2.    An essay about the qualities of kindness.

3.    An essay about the reasons for doing volunteer work.

4.    An essay that describes a Thanksgiving dinner at an American home.

5.    An essay which supports more bicycle lanes in your city.

6.    An essay about the effects of insomnia.

7.    An essay about the qualities of a good speech.

8.    An essay which advocates shortening the regular work week from 40 to 30 hours.

9.    An essay about the different kinds of people who go to the zoo.

10.   An essay which is against the drinking age of 21 years.

## Formatting Your Paper

**Fonts**

If you are typing your paper on a computer, select a font which is easily legible and of appropriate size (12 point). The Geneva or New York fonts are modern, not too small, and easy to read, for example:

*Geneva 12-point:*

He thought he saw an Elephant,
    That practised on a fife:

*New York 12-point:*

He looked again, and found it was
    A letter from his wife.

Please use the same font at 12-point size for your <u>whole paper</u>, including the title. Do not use bold lettering, italics, or shadow lettering, such as the following, in your paper.

Don't type this:     *Gee, isn't this cool?*

or this:     **Wow, this is really smashing!!!!!!!**

**Margins**

Leave a one inch margin on **all sides** of your paper. Set your margins on the computer before you begin typing.

**Spacing**

Always use double-spacing when typing a paper. Select the double-space option from the menu bar on your computer before you begin typing the paper. Everything on the title page should also be double-spaced.

Type only on **one side** of the page.

**Title Page**

The first page of your paper should include the following information: your name, the name of your instructor, the course you are writing the paper for, and date (all in the top left corner); your last name and page number (in the top right corner); the title of your paper (centered); the introductory paragraph, with thesis statement; and the beginning of the rest of your essay.

Here is an example of the top part of a title page:

Garduno 1

Isabel Garduno

Ms. Janet Leamy

ESOL 262: Level 8 Academic Writing

31 July 2007

Reaching Out of Poverty

Would you survive earning less than five dollars per day? Is it impossible to believe that one family can survive with this ridiculous amount of money? However, in Mexico more than thirty percent of the population live in extreme poverty; that is, many families only eat one time a day, live in houses built of rock or cardboard, sometimes without a ceiling, and of course without any essential services (water, electricity, sewer). A few years ago, I belonged to a youth group; one of our activities was to collect clothes, toys and food to take to poorer people that lived in little towns of my city. A lot of enthusiastic people awaited our arrival because they wanted to get old pants, shoes or

**Pagination**

You should number all pages in the upper right-hand corner, 1/2 inch from the top and 1 inch from the right margin. Use the header function on your word-processing software to insert your page numbers.

Type your last name before the page number, in case your pages are lost, for example:

Nguyen 4

# Writing Drafts

It probably takes at least three drafts to write a good paper.

## 1. The rough draft

Start writing your paper with the outline and the notes in front of you. Don't worry too much about your language in this draft. Just try to get all your ideas down on paper in an organized form. Once you have completed the rough draft, you can go back and correct errors. Right now, the most important point to remember is to check your **organization**.

## 2. The second draft

Rewrite the paper and type it, using a computer word-processing program, making sure that organization and most language problems are corrected. Please type double-spaced and follow the proper form for a typed paper (see "Title page", p. 23). If you are writing a research paper, be sure that you have the **correct references** for any quoting or paraphrasing you may have done. This will probably be the first draft that you hand in to your instructor.

## 3. The final draft

Review your instructor's corrections and comments. Correct **any additional errors** and make your final adjustments. Retype the paper.

---

## <u>Review of steps in preparing a paper</u>

| | |
|---|---|
| I. | **Brainstorm and select a topic.** |
| II. | **Narrow the topic.** |
| III. | **Write an outline.** |
| IV. | **Prepare the thesis statement.** |
| V. | **Write the rough draft, with introduction, body paragraphs, and conclusion.** |
| VI. | **Correct the rough draft and type a second draft to hand in to your instructor.** |
| VII. | **Revise and type the final draft, paying close attention to your instructor's comments.** |
| | **You should also have the opportunity to conference with your instructor about at least two of the papers that you write for the class.** |

## Checklist for first draft of essay

Use this checklist to remind yourself to review all of these aspects before handing in your essay.

A.  Format

- ☐  margins (1" all round)
- ☐  pages numbered with last name
- ☐  regular, 12-point font
- ☐  name, instructor name, class, date at top left (double-spaced)
- ☐  title is centered with correct capitalization
- ☐  paragraphs are indented
- ☐  entire essay is double-spaced

B.  Content

- ☐  short, catchy title
- ☐  interesting introduction (anecdote, statistics)
- ☐  clear, specific thesis statement at end of introductory paragraph
- ☐  topic sentence for each body paragraph
- ☐  interesting details and examples for each body paragraph
- ☐  clear and coherent expression of all ideas
- ☐  details in paragraphs relate directly to topic sentence
- ☐  short, meaningful conclusion
- ☐  essay develops from thesis statement

C.  Structure and mechanics

Correct use of:

- ☐  punctuation (commas, sentence fragments, quoted speech)
- ☐  capitalization
- ☐  spelling
- ☐  sentence structure (subject and verb in every sentence)
- ☐  verb tenses (present vs. past tense, present perfect)
- ☐  verb forms (-s ending, passive voice, helping verbs, modals, gerunds, infinitives)
- ☐  word forms
- ☐  prepositions
- ☐  articles
- ☐  conjunctions
- ☐  singular/plural of nouns
- ☐  transition words (*therefore, however, moreover*, etc.)

# RHETORICAL STYLES

## Description Essay

A description essay can be <u>objective</u> or <u>subjective</u>. An objective description describes what anybody can experience. It contains facts, not value judgments or emotions. A subjective description is an individual impression: It conveys the feelings and opinions of the writer.

Follow these points when writing a description:

1. Your introductory paragraph should set the time, place, personalities, and <u>main idea</u> of your description.

2. When you describe a person, place, or object, you want the reader to be able to <u>experience</u> your topic through your writing.

3. Select a topic which is narrow: for example, instead of writing about a city, describe the Saturday market in the city, or better still, one or two stalls at the market; instead of describing an entire house, write only about the balcony or the back yard.

4. A good description has many specific details. The details should be arranged in some kind of order and the description should be cohesive: that is, all the details should relate to each other in some way. Your perceptions, or point of view, should be clear. Dynamics, or movement, in your description should not be confusing.

5. Don't try to describe everything about your topic. Be <u>selective</u>: choose only those aspects which are interesting and which are related to your <u>main idea</u>.

6. In a good description, the writer should attempt to appeal to some of the five senses: **sight, smell, touch, hearing,** and **taste.** Try to evoke colors, odors, emotions.How does light, or time of day, affect the mood or atmosphere? What does a color, odor, sound, or a certain light suggest or symbolize to you?

7. Use metaphors and similes, for example:
"The wheel squeaked like an excited mouse." (simile)
"The sea was a maddened warrior striking out recklessly at a hidden enemy." (metaphor)
"Her skin was hard and wrinkled like a dried fig." (simile)
"The evening's soft, comforting blanket settled on the land, and the wind fell asleep in the oaks." (metaphor)

8. Use past tenses when describing a scene from your past. Use present tenses when describing a place that you continue to visit or use. Always use the past when describing events which have been completed.

9.      Use a variety of adjectives and action verbs.

10.     Your essay should have a controlling idea or message which may be best presented in the conclusion.  Why did you choose this topic?  What special meaning does it have for you?  Your main idea should be briefly mentioned in the introduction (thesis statement).

## Topics for descriptive writing

A description essay often tells a story, usually from the past. Thus, it will have many aspects of a narrative or process essay, but it will be illustrated by many descriptive details and anecdotes. A descriptive essay may also simply describe a scene in great detail. Possible topics might include:

A childhood activity, such as having a snowball fight
An interesting experience described as a sequence of events
The story of an interesting trip
A favorite natural place, scene, or view
A place from your childhood, such as your grandmother's house
An interesting place, such as a crowded bar or disco
An interesting building, bridge, room, etc.
An aspect of a traditional ceremony from your culture
A religious ritual
A modern ceremony, such as graduation
A holiday event
How to perform a complicated task, e.g. prepare for a party, write a novel, rehearse for a
        role in a play, judge a fashion show, prepare for a mountain-climbing expedition,
        hunt a wild animal, do some kind of farm work.

Your instructor will usually set a specific topic, for example:

Describe a favorite place from your childhood.

Describe a ceremony, or part of a ceremony, that you attended.

Describe your favorite vacation spot.

**Description: Using Specific Words**

In order to make your writing more interesting, try to use very specific words.

Vague, general sentence:        We saw some nice things in the shop.

Specific and focused:        We noticed some large, colorful cookbooks arranged tidily on a display table in Annie Bloom's Bookstore.

<u>Exercise 10</u>

Rewrite the following sentences using interesting vocabulary and more specific words. Add adjectives and adverbs where you can.

1.     We ate some good food at a restaurant.

2.     At sunrise, we heard the birds sing.

3.     He was driving a nice-looking car.

4.     The old person walked slowly down the road.

5.     The moon appeared over the tops of the trees.

6.     The truck moved down the road.

7.     A person was in front of the building.

8.     We had an exciting time at a party.

9.     It was a nice day.

10.    She was wearing a beautiful dress.

Exercise 11

Finish the following sentences using your own similes and metaphors. Try to be creative, but also try to use images that other people would understand. See the examples in number 7 on page 30.

Similes

1.  She laughed like

2.  His father drove like

3.  The band played like

4.  The bride looked like

5.  The student was as nervous as

6.  He was as calm as

7.  The bird sang as sweetly as

Metaphors

8.  The clouds

9.  The forest

10. The teacher

11. The ocean

12. The snake

**Name:** _____

## Description Essay: Peer Review

(You may use this exercise to review your own essay, one of your classmate's essays or one of the essays on pp. 37-39)

**Writer:** _____

**Title:** _____

1.   What is the topic of the essay?

2.   Is the focus of the essay narrow enough, or do you think the author should narrow the topic more? Do you have any suggestions?

3.   Does the writer get your attention in the introduction? Why/Why not?

4.   Write down two or three similes or metaphors that the writer uses.

5.   What is the best part of the essay? Why?

6.   What is the least effective aspect of this essay? How do you suggest that the writer change it?

7.   On the back of this sheet, write a paragraph which details your response to this essay.

# Description Essay: Example #1

## An Unforgettable Trip

While waiting to pick up a close friend recently at Union Station, I was reminded of an unforgettable train trip that my mother and I took in 1981 to visit my father, who was living in a re-education camp in northern Vietnam. Our trip from Binh Trieu Station to my father's camp taught me the strength of my mother's love for my father through hard, strange, and stressful times.

On December 20th, my mother and I carefully packed rice, sugar, salt, milk, meat, and several kinds of dried fish to take to my father, who was being held in Hanoi. Early that morning, we rushed off to Binh Trieu, a small train station near my house in southern Vietnam. After buying two tickets, we got on the train, found two seats, and stored our luggage. It took us almost four days to get to Hanoi, arriving in the evening.

When we got to this city, which we had never visited before, we felt like fish out of water. After getting off the train, most of the other passengers quickly dispersed because they knew exactly where they wanted to go. We, on the other hand, felt lost because we didn't know how to get to my father's camp or what transportation we should take. Then a man standing beside a motorcycle with a small trailer attached came up and asked my mother, "Where are you going?" When my mother explained that we were going to visit my father at Hanoi's re-education camp, he smiled and said, "Don't worry. I'll take both of you. It takes about two hours." He helped us put our luggage into the trailer. Finally, we arrived at my father's camp at midnight, and my mother paid the driver.

We were taken to a cottage that had no furniture or electricity. There were some candles burning on the walls. The air in this low-roofed cottage was very humid. Over thirty people were waiting there to visit husbands, sons, or other relatives. Because of the long trip, we were quite tired, so we fell asleep on the ground almost immediately. The next morning, the director of the camp came and told my mother that we had to wait at least three days to see my father, that we could see him for only one hour, and that it was an annoyance for him to have to arrange for visits on such short notice.

My mother and I were deeply disappointed, but we waited and slept in the cottage without blankets. The evenings were cool and the nights rather cold. As a result, I got sick, and my mother had to stay up at night to take care of me. My mother expected me to improve, but I only got worse, so she cried and requested that the director allow us to visit my father sooner than scheduled. Finally, he reluctantly agreed.

I had tried to imagine my father's appearance and voice, but it was hard because I hadn't seen him for eight years. Although I was sick, I sat up in a chair in a small room beside the cottage waiting with my mother to see my father. At the same time, seven other women and four other children were sitting around waiting for their relatives. Everyone was silent; we just looked at each other without talking. Suddenly, the door opened. Eight men stepped in and sat down face to face with their wives, children, and friends. At that important moment, my father, who was thin with darkened skin, sat opposite us. My parents looked at each other but didn't talk for a while. When I looked around, I saw other people looking at each other without speaking. My parents had tears in their eyes. My father held and kissed my mother's hand. A little later, my father held me tightly, kissed me on the forehead, and asked me many everyday questions such as, "How are you? Have you been good? How is school? What are you doing in your leisure time? Did you go somewhere last summer?" He listened to every single answer, touched my face, and reminded me of something he always included in his letters: "You must obey your mother and help her in any way you can and not forget to write to me whenever you have time."

I was deeply moved by my father's appearance, voice, and words. The visiting hour went by so fast that I couldn't believe it. However, I felt very satisfied and happy to have seen my father. After that, my mother kept visiting my father twice a year until he was released on June 8, 1987. My family came to the United States in 1993. Since then, my father has been working for an electric company, and my mother has been staying home taking care of my father, brother, older sister, and me. I'm often reminded of our amazing trip and the strength of my parents' love. I thank God for giving me wonderful parents who never stopped believing in their future.

**Kim Dang**

# Description Essay: Example #2

### My Last Climb

On a sunny Sunday afternoon, my day off from school, I began to act as a typical twelve-year-old tomboy. I went around my yard to choose a tree that was worthy for me to climb, "Okay, guava seems to be the best," I declared eagerly. I went around examining the tree with my hands on my hips, eyes narrowed, and my head nodding. I started to climb the tree, and a painful story was born.

A light wind was shaking the guava branches as if it was daring my courage, but I didn't care. I started by taking my shoes off. Rubbing my hands together while walking with anticipation to the tree's base, I thought of the sweet guavas. After I held the trunk in my two hands, I climbed to the top of the tree. I looked down at the ground and at my little black dog, who was waving his tail rapidly, and then I laughed in victory.

"Ha-ha! I am the heroine of the twentieth century!" I shouted at the top of my lungs.

Suddenly, an enormous wind came and shook the tree so wildly that my right hand couldn't even hold on to any of its branches. I was too excited to feel scared about falling. However, the terrible event didn't stop there. As my right hand was trying to catch one of those branches, I didn't notice the nearby ant nest. When I clumsily touched that ant nest, hundreds of ants ran out of their nest to swarm over my hand. My hand was covered by so many ants that it looked like a dirty black floor. One by one, the ants attacked me. I was so scared that I could not think of how to get rid of those evil ants. My panic grew greater, and I almost started to cry. "What can I do? What can I do?" I thought in fear. Furthermore, with my hand, which was covered by ants, I negligently touched my eyes, and one of the ants ran into my left eye. It bit and sprayed fluid into my eye. This time tears flowed out of my eyes for real.

"Aaaaaaaaaaaa! Someone, please help me! Aaaaaaaaaaaaaa! Help! Help! Help!" I screamed in horror. My little dog barked crazily as if he knew what was going on. My eye hurt so much that I couldn't open it. I decided to climb down the tree with my eyes closed. My hands and feet groped to find a way to get down. I didn't hear my dad's voice until I got to the ground.

"Phuong, what's going on? What happened to you? What did you do?" Question after question poured from my dad hurriedly.

"I climbed, hic, the guava, hic, my hand, hic, touched, hic, the ant nest, hic, the ants bit, hic, my eye, hic, I hurt, hic, hic," I answered incoherently while sobbing.

My dad took my arm and led me to my house. A little while later, my dad hugged me and took me to the hospital. The doctor there gave me some medicine. My eye was red for some days afterward, and I had to take eye drops, but luckily for me, it was not so bad that I would be blind.

Since the dreadful event, I have never climbed trees again. I am so scared to test my bravery anymore. Furthermore, the ant species has been added to my list of enemies. It was an important lesson for me to become a normal girl. Now that I am older, I tell my friends this story to entertain them and to remind me not to be mischievous.

**Anh-Phuong Nguyen**

# Classification Essay

Classification is the process of grouping together people or things that are alike in some way. A simple classification would be to classify cars in terms of their body size: full-size, mid-size, compacts, and sub-compacts, or Portland Community College in terms of its different campuses. These groups or categories, are helpful in letting you see relationships among people or objects. They help you to organize information and compare it.

However, these categories often do not exist in the real world; they may exist only in your mind. You create them using some criterion or organizing principle. For example, you can classify college students by looking at their study habits: those who schedule study time, those who cram before a test, and those who hardly study at all. The organizing principle for classifying students in the example above is the different ways that they study. On the other hand, you could just as easily have classified students according to their age, their grade point average, or their religion. You could just as easily have classified cars according to their cost, their gas mileage, or their body style.

If you want your categories to be clear and consistent when you create a classification, make sure that you follow these two rules:

1.  Use only one criterion or <u>organizing principle</u> so that everyone or everything fits into only one category, for example:

    Group people according to income, or intelligence, or industriousness-- but

    not according to income and intelligence, or intelligence and....

2.  Create categories that allow room for everyone or everything you are classifying

## Topic selection

Classification essays are commonly used in business, science, advertising, and editorials. However, at this level, a classification essay can be <u>subjective</u>. Sometimes classification essays are humorous or sarcastic. Choose a topic of interest to you and your audience. Use your imagination. Have fun, be creative, and be original -- the structure is straightforward.

You will have to write a <u>thesis statement</u> which you will then have to support in the details of the essay. An example of an appropriate thesis statement might be:

> **Girls have various ways of choosing boyfriends based on their desire for money, love or common interest.**

The body of the essay should explore the qualities of each category, with clear examples and anecdotes.

Suggestions for topics:

**People:**        husbands, wives, in-laws, teachers, students, friends, enemies, bosses, co-workers, doctors, nurses, patients, babies, ex-wives, ex-husbands, grandparents, teenagers, mothers, fathers, lawyers, secretaries, T.V. news announcers, hairstylists, book lovers, ice-cream eaters, umbrella users, disco dancers, market vendors, Beanie Baby collectors, etc.

**Places:**        vacation spots, campgrounds, tutoring centers, college campuses, airports, freeways, back yards, front porches, parks, gardens, vegetable plots, video game arcades, movie theaters, Chinese restaurants, car washes, hiking trails, etc.

**Habits:**        lunch habits, morning routines, test-taking, jogging, T.V. watching, bus riding, letter writing, dishwashing, house cleaning, house painting, playing, changing diapers, taking a shower, etc.

**Occasions:**    weddings, funerals, birthday parties, Christmas celebrations, dinner parties, commencements, company meetings, family picnics, Mother's Day celebrations, vacations, reunions, etc.

Your instructor will probably set you a topic area from which you need to make your own topic selection.

**Some advice:**

1.      At this level, don't choose topics that are already obvious to the reader. For example, don't write about the four levels of college students (freshmen, sophomores, juniors, and seniors) or the three branches of government (legislative, executive, judicial). You should try to be original and creative in your selection of a topic.

2.      Remember that you should have a rationale for your categories. Think about your life experiences. Do you want to make a social comment or give advice? For example, imagine that you just got out of the hospital after a long stay. You noticed that there was a wide range in the quality of nursing care, so you decide to categorize nurses according to the way they treat their patients; or you have worked for various lawn service companies, so you are able to categorize them for the reader.

3.      Make sure that your categories can be clearly labeled, for example: "helpful husbands, unhelpful husbands, and reluctant husbands" **NOT** "helpful husbands, unhelpful husbands, and the ones in the middle."

**Examples of Classification essay outlines**

| Topic | Organizing principle | Categories |
|---|---|---|
| **Rhythmic gymnasts on the team in Maringa, Brazil** | Their interest in joining the team | 1. Some were addicted to practice and hard work. <br> 2. Others liked the social aspect. <br> 3. The others wanted to travel. |
| **Hiking trails** | Their condition | 1. Some are maintained regularly. <br> 2. Some get intermittent care. <br> 3. Others are kept open only by other hikers. <br> 4. The others have been abandoned. |
| **Residents of an adult foster care home** | Their attitudes about exercising | 1. Some refuse to exercise and rely on their medications. <br> 2. Others exercise only when they need to "cure" a problem. <br> 3. The others take exercise very seriously. |
| **Children's birthday parties** | Types of entertainment | 1. The children are left to play by themselves. <br> 2. Parents and other adults organize games. <br> 3. An entertainer is hired to come to the party. <br> 4. The party is held at a location which has many activities that cost money. |
| **Cleaning the house** | Thoroughness | 1. The total cleaning – everything top to bottom <br> 2. The vacuum job only <br> 3. Spot cleaning: only the places that look dirty |
| **Homestay families** | Why they want foreign students to stay with them | 1. Some do it just for the money. <br> 2. Others are really interested in helping and learning from a foreign student. <br> 3. The others are lonely and want a companion. |

**Name:** _____

## Classification Essay:  Peer Review

(You may use this exercise to review your own essay, one of your classmate's essays or one of the essays on pp. 45-48)

Title:       _____

Writer:     _____

1.    Write the thesis statement below.  What are the categories the author is describing?

2.    Does the writer give equal space to each category or group?  If not, please comment.

3.    Is each body paragraph developed with sufficient detail?

4.    In your opinion, what is the best part of this essay, and why?

5.    Which part of this essay is the least effective?  How would you suggest that the writer change it?

6.    On the back of this sheet, write a response to your classmate's classification essay.

# Classification Essay: Example #1

## Many Ways to Turn a Page

People say that one can understand a lot about someone's personality just by looking at his shoes. The way people take care of their shoes reveals a lot about their characters. Similarly, the way people treat their books can be definitive about a reader's personality. Therefore, most readers could fall into one of five groups: the perfectionist, the teacher, the antiquarian, the collector, and the aesthete.

If one happens to be in a bookstore and sees someone asking the bookseller for a copy that has never been opened before, this person must be a perfectionist. People in this category are usually very fastidious about everything, including their books. Book lovers in this category are most likely to go to a shelf in a bookstore and spend hours exploring the contents of books before they choose one. After they choose a book, they will ask for an immaculate copy - if it is possible, never touched by a hand - and for sure they will check for misprints, folded pages and may ask that the tag with the price be peeled off (if there is one). They use their books in the same manner. They probably read their books at a 45-degree angle, so that they look as if they have never been read. A perfectionist will never write on his books, and he will shelve them in perfect thematic order. Of course, his shoes always look blindingly polished.

The next category of readers is the teachers. People in this category are usually life-long readers and use books as a tool for gaining knowledge. For them, the book as an object doesn't have as much value as the book as a source of information, knowledge, and ideas. The teacher most likely will write on his books, since for him they are not sacred objects of adoration, but just useful tools for sharing ideas. His beliefs, ideas, and positions can be seen in the remarks made in the margins. Usually people from this category have a very accurate ability to distinguish significant things from marginal ones. Like the perfectionist, the teacher will put his books in thematic order, but he will always care more about the knowledge inside them instead of the books themselves. The teacher is a kind of reader who easily will share his books with other people because he actually enjoys sharing ideas. Moreover, he wouldn't care if some of his books were lost, since he has already read them.

The third category is the antiquarian. This category is very specific. People who have an antiquarian interest in books should be called book lovers, rather than readers. Of course, they like to read books, but their main attitude toward books is expressed generally in the possession of books as objects with commercial value. These people have a wide bibliographic knowledge about books. For example, they know about publishers, different editions, years of publication, copies, and reprints. People in this category are "book hunters". Sometimes they dedicate their whole life to the passion of finding rare books; as a result, they make this interest about books their profession. Most of them are bookstore owners since they evaluate books mainly as objects with a high commercial value. The antiquarian reminds me of a *souteneur* (a pimp) : he loves books, but more than that, he loves the money he gains from them.

The collectors are a different group of book lovers. How is this category different from those already mentioned? On the one hand, it looks pretty close to the antiquarian; on the other hand, it has a lot in common with the teacher. Thus, it seems that this category of people is somehow in between these two others. While the antiquarian likes to collect books with a commercial interest, the collector has a 100% personal interest. This is the main difference. The collector, like the teacher, evaluates books according to the knowledge he can find through them. However, instead of gaining this knowledge, he buys books with the idea to read them later, at some future moment. This way he makes huge collections of books that he doesn't read for years, sometimes even never. The collector enjoys reading, but since he doesn't have time to read, he develops a dependence on the possession of books. In other words the collector is "a put–off–teacher" and not a real antiquarian.

Finally, the last category of book lovers is the aesthete. People from this category can be called "readers" only in a formal sense. Actually, they don't like to read at all, but they have specific attitudes toward books. These are people who see books as a nice way to add comfort, a good look or the "last detail" to their magazine–style interior. Books in their world exist along with vases, family pictures, boxes, and candles. The most important quality that book can have in such a world is a pretty cover matching the interior style. For the aesthete, books have value only as a decoration. They are nothing more than a needed accent, so that the interior vision looks complete. For example, the aesthete often buys book collections only to fill the empty shelves, so the room can look cozy. The aesthete will rarely open a book, but will regularly clean the dust from it as a part of the furniture.

In conclusion, it can be seen that books are like signs reflecting people's personalities; indeed, books are a very significant factor expressing someone's personal values. Since the scripts of antiquity until today, books have changed their image many times, but they have always had a significant role as cultural icons. Maybe soon books will have mostly a virtual existence; however, the attitude toward reading will still reveal one's personal philosophy.

**Andriana Yovcheva**

# Classification essay: Example #2

## First Families

"My host family took me to the beach yesterday. It was so nice!"

"Really? I envy you! My host family doesn't even feed me well!"

There are sometimes these kinds of conversations among the international students. Many international students, especially those who stay in America for a short time, prefer to stay with an American host family because they can experience American culture, and it is helpful to improve their English. However, not all international students get to stay with a pleasant host family. Having talked about host families with several of my acquaintances, I realized that there are different reasons why American host families invite an international student.

The first type of American host family is the host family who invites an international student because of money. Of course, this is one of the basic reasons why most American host families invite international students. However, this type of host family's purpose is only to earn money from an international student. When I studied in a private English academy, I met a student who was living with that kind of host family. She paid more than $500 per month, but they'd never offered her good food. They always gave her only a slice of bread or a small portion of frozen food. She'd never seen milk or fruit in her host family's house. When she asked her host mother to give one more slice of bread, her host mother even answered no. Another student whom I met was living in a bad environment. For example, there was no lamp in his room and no telephone in his house. Of course, this type of host family doesn't treat its host students well, and they don't try to take care of their host students.

The second type of American host family is the host family who really wants to help international students. In the city where I am living now, there is a Christian group organized to help international students. All members in this Christian group try to help international students by offering a volunteer tutoring service or making a party for international students. Also, some members invite host students, and most of the students who find their host family in this group are satisfied with their family. Because their main goal is to help international students, these families don't receive much money from their students. They treat their students well, and try to help their host students to live in America, which is a very strange country for them. In my case, I also found a host family by contacting this group, and they were very helpful people. They gave me a lot of information about the area, like the locations of important buildings or the way to use public transportation. Also, they tried to make me experience American culture, so my host parents took me to a potluck party or invited me to a family dinner. Whenever I asked about English expressions, American customs, or my homework, they tried to help me in any way they could.

The third type of host family is the family who invites international students to stay out of their own loneliness. This is usually a family consisting of a retired couple or a single person. Some people feel lonely after retirement and have nothing to do, especially if their house is an empty nest. Therefore, therefore they host an international student and treat the international student like their real daughter or son. This also applies to people who live alone. One of my friends who came to

America to learn English lived with this kind of host mother. The host mother was divorced, and she wanted to host a student because she was lonely living alone. Therefore, she treated my friend like a real daughter. She took my friend everywhere she went and introduced my friend whenever they met new people. When my friend returned to her home after class, she and her host mother made dinner together, watched TV and talked for a long time.

    Living with an American host family has many advantages. Especially for foreign students, having the experience of living with a host family is a huge support. However, whether the experience is pleasant or not depends on the attitudes of the students as well as the attitudes of the families themselves. Therefore, I hope international students living in America can meet host families who will enrich their experiences in this country and leave them with pleasant memories.

**Hae Yeon Cho**

# Definition Essay

A definition essay goes beyond just a dictionary definition of a word. Usually a word or concept can be defined in just one sentence. A definition essay, however, needs to be several paragraphs. Therefore, the definition must be extended to include examples, details, personal experience, description, causes, effects, analysis, etc.

Above all, a definition essay must demonstrate a detailed account of your own opinion about the word or concept. For example, if you are writing an essay about "love," the thesis and the details must be based upon your personal ideas of what "love" is.

Topics for definition essays are always general. In other words, you can write about "Love" or "Truth" or "Justice," but not "My love for my wife" or "The truth about violence on T.V." Definition essays are also subjective: you need to assert and support your own opinions about the concept.

Definition essays have two basic parts:

1. The denotation, or <u>direct explanation</u> of the meaning, and

2. The connotation, or the ideas that the word <u>implies</u> or includes.

   For example, you may say that "love" means "an affection for a person or thing" (denotation). However, what does the word "love" imply? Does it imply loyalty, dedication, gift-giving, sexual passion (connotation)? Do any of these not mean "love" for you? You can check in a thesaurus for words of similar meanings that may show connotations.

<u>Topics for a definition essay</u>

Your instructor should set a certain topic or topic area.

I. Abstract concepts

   Define one of the following (or another abstract concept):

| | | |
|---|---|---|
| Truth | Love | Hatred |
| Justice | Honor | Loyalty |
| Fidelity | Courage | Cowardice |
| Liberty | Prejudice | Tolerance |
| Greed | Ambition | Generosity |
| Self-confidence | Pride | Modesty |
| Sensitivity | Insensitivity | Boredom |
| Adventure | Good taste | Poor taste |

These could also be defined as adjectives, e.g. "A proud person" or "An ambitious person."

Additionally, you could define a concept from your own culture or language for which we don't have an equivalent in English. When writing a word from your own language, always use italics. here are some examples of words from other languages for which we have no exact equivalent in English:

| | | |
|---|---|---|
| *ataoso* | Spanish | one who sees problems with everything |
| *giomlaireachd* | Scots Gaelic | the habit of visiting others at meal times |
| *termangu-mangu* | Indonesian | sad and not sure what to do |
| *ichigo-ichie* | Japanese | the practice of tryng to make each moment perfect |
| *lagom* | Swedish | not too much and not too little; the right amount |

II.    Good or Bad

Define a "good" or "bad" one of the following (e.g. "a good friend" or "a bad vacation.")

| | | |
|---|---|---|
| **Friend** | **Marriage** | **Teacher** |
| **Job** | **Husband** | **Wife** |
| **Child** | **Class** | **Vacation** |
| **Meeting** | **Date** | **Home** |

Begin your brainstorming by asking yourself "What are the qualities of a good class?" or "What is prejudice?" Then think of examples, facts, anecdotes, personal experiences, opposites, etc. that can help to define your topic.

III.    A Place

Define a specific place in terms of its special qualities and what it means to you. These could be both positive and negative qualities. The place could be as large as a country or as small as a room.

| | |
|---|---|
| **Country** | **(e.g. Armenia)** |
| **State** | **(e.g. Utah)** |
| **City** | **(e.g. Los Angeles)** |
| **Small Town** | **(e.g. Hood River)** |
| **Neighborhood** | **(e.g. Greenwich Village)** |
| **Shopping area** | **(e.g. a local mall)** |
| **Park** | **(e.g. Hyde Park, London)** |
| **Street** | **(e.g. 5th Avenue, New York)** |
| **House** | **(e.g. your grandmother's house)** |
| **Room** | **(e.g. your kitchen)** |

Choose a place which is familiar to you and about which you have many ideas and impressions.

**Organizational pattern for definition essay**:

**1st paragraph:**

    Introduction:    "hook" -
                      anecdote, interesting facts,
                      humorous story, personal experience

    Thesis statement: topic + your definition

**Body paragraphs:**

    Begin each paragraph with a topic sentence.

    Develop body paragraphs in some of these ways:

    a) analyze:        divide into parts and define each part;
    b) compare:       show similarities and/or differences with
                      other ideas;
    c) exemplify:     use examples to illustrate each body paragraph;
    d) negate:        define what the topic is not so you can clarify
                      what it is;
    e) illustrate:     describe the subject in detail, giving specific
                      information;
    f) give background: relate the history of the word or idea;

**Conclusion:**

    Summary, prediction, anecdote, comparison, etc.

**Name:** _____

## Definition Essay:  Peer Review
(You may use this exercise to review your own essay, one of your classmate's essays or one of the essays on pp. 55-57)

Title:       _____

Writer:       _____

1.       Write the thesis statement below.  What are the qualities the author is defining?

2.       Does the writer give equal space to each quality?  If not, please comment.

3.       Is each body paragraph developed in sufficient detail?

4.       In your opinion, what is the best part of this essay, and why?

5.       Which part of this essay is the least effective?  How would you suggest that the writer change it?

6.       On the back of this sheet, write a response to your classmate's definition essay.

# Definition Essay: Example #1

## *Ishindenshin*

*Ishindenshin* is a common Japanese word. It describes a Japanese concept used to refer to communication without words or a "reading of the heart." We Japanese do not always say exactly what we think or feel. People can guess and receive what is in a sender's heart. People can understand each other without words. This is not a familiar concept in western cultures, where people are generally encouraged to state exactly what they mean. The phenomenon of *ishindenshin* works well when Japanese are communicating in Japan, but it can present certain challenges when Japanese are communicating outside of their country.

*Ishindenshin* was born as a Buddhist word. The story goes that when Buddha preached to a lot of disciples about Buddhism, it was too hard to express the depth of the religion in words, so he showed them a lotus flower to communicate a point. Although most of his disciples could not understand what he meant, there was one who could understand. After that, Buddha preached his teachings only to the enlightened disciple instead of to many disciples.

There are many ways that Japanese demonstrate *ishindenshin* in their daily lives. For example, when people ride on a bus, they stand up and give their seats to someone who is old or has a physical disability. *Ishindenshin* works especially well in situations like this where people do not know one another. It is like telepathy because people do not say anything. In Japanese culture, we seldom say negative words to other people because we are observant about hurting someone, but non-verbal communication will often get a negative point across. For example, my mother often has a sore shoulder. When she does, she shakes her head a takes a few deep breaths. At this point, all of us in the family know what she wants us to do, so she gets a massage.

*Ishindenshin* is a very useful concept. Understanding each other without explaining feelings is a convenient tool in communication. However, at the same time, it does sometimes cause misunderstandings. When I came to the United States the first time when I was 13, an American family welcomed me into their home as a family member. When I felt hungry and wanted to get something to eat, I expressed my feelings with the words, "I am beginning to get hungry," but my host mother did not give me anything to eat. I felt so strange. Even though my English was not good, I knew that I had said the words clearly. I thought that she was so mean and did not want to give me any food, especially when my host sister got snacks for her and not for me. Then I thought about whether there was something wrong with my communication and decided to ask her directly for something to eat. I learned that there was no *ishindenshin* in American culture, so I had to say exactly what I wanted. I realized that outside of my own country, I had to adjust my communication style.

A Japanese overseas study coordinator that I know said that Japanese students may not be as good at English as many other international students because they are accustomed to the concept of *ishindenshin*. He also said that it is very hard for Japanese students to express every idea that they wish to communicate. There are many differences between the cultures of the U.S. and

Japan; however, to know new things about other cultures is very interesting, so Japanese living in other countries need to get accustomed to talking in different ways.

*Ishindenshin* has mostly good effects but can also have a few bad ones for Japanese living outside of their country. Using this telepathy too much can have unfortunate consequences, but I believe it is important to use a moderate amount. We sometimes have to use our emotional intelligence and interpret feelings without words because there are situations in all people's lives when there are no words to express exactly how we feel.

**Chisako Hayakawa**

## Definition Essay: Example #2

### A Good Husband

"I love you so much!" my elementary school friend said to my husband, and she kissed my husband's lips. After we came out of her house, I urged my husband to answer my questions. "What was that? Why did she do that? What relationship is between two of you?" My husband answered that there was nothing, and that my friend was lonely because she had just become alone. I shouted toward my husband, "Are you protecting her, now?" My husband raised his voice to me, " Why are you shouting at me? I told you there was nothing between your friend and me!" I got angry so much that I took my stuff and rushed out of my house. I shouted, "I can't live with you any more!" But he didn't even try to stop me and let me go. I couldn't believe what was happening to me. I was going crazy, I yelled "Ah a a a k!!" With a scream I woke up and saw that my husband was sleeping beside me with his usual snore. I thanked God that it was just a terrible dream. He may not be perfect but at least he does not have an affair with my friend. What makes a good husband? I think a good husband should be a best friend who should be respected by his wife and be sincere to his married life.

A good husband should be a best friend to his wife. When a man and a woman meet and fall in love, they feel that they can do everything with their burning love. However, after marriage they can find themselves in reality and realize that their burning love is not eternal. They might find each other's weak points and become disappointed. They also might try to fit their spouse into their own personality under the name of love. However even when married, if you have a mindset of being best friends, that could give more serenity of mind to each other than lovers because they respect each other's privacy. A good husband, like a good friend, acknowledges his wife's weak points and accepts those as her personality. Also a good husband will respect his wife's sense of value, emotion, thoughts and desires like a friend.

*denotation*

A good husband should have his wife's respect. For the wife, respecting her husband is sometimes more important than loving her husband because a woman can't keep on loving her husband without first respecting him. It doesn't mean a good husband has to be very successful in his life. Most men think making a lot of money is the only way to make their wives happy. Making a lot of money is important, but it is not everything. A woman can be satisfied with just a rose from her husband. Like that, a wife's emotional satisfaction is just as important. If a husband makes less money than other men, but his wife respects and is proud of her husband's honesty or sincerity that may be enough for her happiness.

A good husband is sincere to his married life. He must keep his marriage vows. Whether he is happy or going through a hard time, he should always share his feelings with his wife. When trouble comes to him and his wife, he should be patient about solving the problems with his wife, and he never should have an affair with any other woman, of course. Until one of them is dead, he should always love and be faithful to his wife,

A good husband's characteristics are not only suitable for a good husband but also for a good wife. There is no perfect husband and wife. It is impossible. In my case, if I give a grade to my husband, he will get a "C+". If that is true, then what would my grade be? In my country when a couple marry, they swear in such a way, "Until the black hair turns to white...." I think that even though no one is perfect, if you try you will be a good husband. A good husband has an open mind like a friend, should be respected by his wife and sincere to his married life.

Jieun Yoo

# Cause /Effect essay

A cause/effect essay is an explanation of why something happened or why something is happening and/or the results of this event. Some essays focus on causes, others on effects; many discuss both. At this level, you should focus on either causes or effects in detail, but not both in equal measure.

It is important to give careful thought to the planning stage of this essay. Before beginning the composition, list the various causes or effects that occur to you, consider the probability of each one, and decide on the most likely explanation or explanations. When you are not positive that your explanation is accurate, you should use terms like "maybe", "possibly", or "probably".

## <u>Writing the essay</u>

1.  Choose a <u>limited</u> or <u>narrow</u> topic and use your personal knowledge or experience, for example:

           The effect of barking dogs in the neighborhood
    NOT  The causes of world overpopulation

2.  Think of at least <u>three</u> causes and/or effects for your topic.

3.  Before beginning the composition, list the various causes or effects that occur to you, consider the probability of each one, and decide on the <u>most likely</u> explanation or explanations. When you are not positive that your explanation is accurate, you should use terms like "maybe", "possibly", or "probably".

4.  Put the <u>least important</u> cause or effect first and the most important last.

5.  Think of interesting <u>details</u> and <u>examples</u> you can give for each cause and/or effect.

6.  Write a <u>thesis statement</u> that shows your topic and your emphasis (causes or effects).

7.  Make sure you have a <u>topic sentence</u> for each of the body paragraphs.

8.  Write an <u>outline</u> that sketches out your main ideas, topic sentences, and the thesis statement.

9.  Think of an interesting <u>introduction</u> for your essay. Use an anecdote, some interesting facts or a personal experience as a "hook" to get the reader interested in the topic.

10.  Think of a suitable <u>conclusion</u>. Your conclusion could summarize the ideas in your essay, make a prediction, state your opinion, etc.

11.  Make sure that your <u>body paragraphs</u> are well-developed.

12.    Use <u>simple present</u> tense for facts (what is still true) and <u>past</u> tense for examples of experiences and things that are no longer true. Use <u>present perfect</u> for changes that began in the past and are still happening. The <u>passive voice</u> is often used in cause/effect essays because the agent may not be known.

13.    Use some of the following transition words, conjunctions, prepositions and subordinating words in your essay. Make sure that you use correct <u>punctuation</u>.

| | | |
|---|---|---|
| therefore | because | so |
| consequently | since | for |
| as a result | now that | |
| thus | as | due to |
| as long as | because of | |
| so . . . that | | |

## Organization

Your essay should be structured as follows:

| | |
|---|---|
| **Introduction:** | Anecdote or definition of topic; brief summary of causes if you are writing an effect essay, or effects if you are writing a cause essay; thesis statement showing whether you are addressing causes or effects. |
| **Body:** | Listing of various causes or effects. Select the most important ones. Use a topic sentence for each paragraph. Support each general statement with details and examples. |
| **Conclusion:** | Short paragraph suggesting a possible solution or prediction. |

## Suggested Topics:

Causes/effects of a particular business trend, e.g. foreign investment
Causes/effects of a particular societal change, e.g. career women in your culture
Reasons for choosing a particular career
Causes/effects of misunderstandings between people of different cultures
Causes/effects of a problem in your native country, e.g. official corruption
Causes (or effects) of an important decision you have made in your life

**Some advice:**

Please do not try to write about broad social problems or medical problems unless you have some expertise in the field. You will not be able to write an essay about "The Effects of Smoking", for example, and make it specific, interesting, and original unless you have already done some in-depth study of the subject. Topics to avoid are the causes or effects of the following:

| | | |
|---|---|---|
| divorce | the homeless | drinking and driving |
| smoking | violent crime in America | alcoholism |
| T.V. violence | teenage pregnancy | the budget deficit |

**Some examples topics for this assignment:**

The household recycling program in Korea (effects)

Wearing a chador in Iran  (effects)

The usefulness of a personal digital assistant (PDA) (effects)

Doing tai chi (effects)

A child's bedwetting problem (causes)

The Internet and travel agencies (effects)

Anxiety about in-class writing tests (causes)

Family pressure to get into a good college in Iran (causes)

Divorce because of friction between mother-in-law and daughter-in-law in Korea (causes)

High infection rate of hospital patients in Vietnam (causes)

Difficulties of parents of Korean teens in the U.S.  (causes)

The secrets of longevity in Okinawa (causes)

Pleasure in playing a musical instrument (effects)

Life as a Palestinian refugee (effects)

Migration from the rural areas to the capital city of Niger, Niamey (effects)

Problems with being a landlord  (causes)

Bullying among school children in Japan  (causes)

**Name:** _____

## Cause/Effect Essay:  Peer Review

(You may use this exercise to review your own essay, one of your classmate's essays or one of the essays on pp. 63-65)

Writer:        _____

Title:          _____

1.       Write the thesis statement of the essay.


2.       What is the topic of each body paragraph?

         A.


         B.


         C.


3.       Are there details and examples in each body paragraph?




4.       What is the best part of this essay? Why?




5.       How do you think the writer could improve this essay?  Give one suggestion
         about how he/she can improve the essay.




6.       On the back of this sheet, write a one-paragraph response to the essay.

# Cause essay

## An Incomplete Education

In the Philippines, we value education very much and sending children to college is an important consideration. Parents prioritize their children's education even to their last penny. We believe that knowledge is wealth and parents are very happy to give it to their kids. The new millennium has presented a lot of challenges to all youths. The workplace is becoming sophisticated and digitized. A college education is even more necessary for a high salary job. Unfortunately, for a variety of reasons, many Filipino college students do not successfully complete their college degree. *thesis*

The most obvious reason for dropping out of college is lack of finances. I finished my bachelor's degree in Hotel and Restaurant Management three years ago at the Lyceum of the Philippines. Without a partial scholarship that I received from the local government, I would have been forced to quit my studies due to limited finances. I would have needed to work to earn money like most of my friends. My friend Grace attended college on and off for seven years because she couldn't afford to pay the school expenses. Last year, she got a job and decided to discontinue her studies. She found it very difficult to study and work at the same time. *cause*

Some students choose to drop out because they want quick and easy money. For example, my former classmate in college, Marilyn, got a job as a bartender in a prestigious five star hotel in Manila just after entering college. After finishing just one semester, she decided to quit her studies. Probably, she still preferred the life she had before and her priority was to work and earn money rather than study in poverty. *cause*

Another factor which causes female students to drop out of college is pregnancy. First comes the often difficult period of pregnancy, which is followed by the full time demands of motherhood. One very good example was our valedictorian in high school, Jacqueline, who got pregnant during her first year in college. She was taking a physical therapy course and dropped out of college because she had a difficult pregnancy. *cause*

Finally, many students lack direction in their studies and frequently change their majors. My brother David had a former classmate in college, Eric, who was taking Aviation Maintenance at PATTS college. He failed three subjects in his first year. That caused him much discouragement, so instead of continuing Aviation, he decided to take computer courses. *cause*

Whether we choose to stay in school or to drop out is ultimately our own decision. It can have a lot to do with the future quality of our lives. Completing an education is one of life's greatest achievements.

**Ruth Zingeser**

## Effect essay

### Domestic Terror Strikes Hard

*cause*

There have been countless historically atrocious crimes. For example, World War I and II involved many countries and many terrible events which occurred during these two wars. In recent years, the September 11th, 2001 attacks in New York City, organized by Islamic terrorists, still live in our memories. These affairs were conflicts among countries and ideologies. However, in 1995, a sarin gas attack by the Japanese cult, Aum Shinrikyo, became the most shocking terrorist act inside Japan. Around 8:00 a.m. on March 20th, 1995, ten believers of Aum Shinrikyo each released a total of one liter of liquid sarin, a poisonous gas used as an agrichemical, which was contained in plastic bags. The believers punctured the bags with the sharp points of their umbrellas in five subway trains in the center of Tokyo. Many passengers collapsed in the trains one after another, after which the trains were stopped, and the passengers became panicky at the stations. The subway sarin incident caused many deaths and injuries, made criminals of the believers, and created confusion in Japan.

*effect*

One result was that a lot of people were hurt by the subway sarin incident. During the peak hours of traffic, one passenger of the Marunouchi Line, one passenger of the Hibiya Line and four passengers of another Hibiya Line died because they could not breathe. A single drop of sarin could kill an adult, and many innocent citizens were exposed to ten liters of sarin. Unfortunately, large numbers of subway users and many station employees and medical staff who tried to help the passengers became victims because they did not have much knowledge about the toxicity of sarin and the appropriate treatments for the poison. For that reason, two station attendants of the Chiyoda Line were killed at Kasumigaseki Station, and eight others of the Hibiya Line were also severely injured by being exposed to the leftover sarin at Kodenma-cho Station. As a result, 5,510 victims in all were injured either slightly or seriously. To make matters worse, some of them still suffer from vision troubles such as declining vision, chronic eyestrain, or post-traumatic stress disorder when they ride subway trains.

*effect*

The second effect was that the followers of Aum Shinrikyo became criminals. Before joining the community, they were also general citizens who commuted to or graduated from high-level universities. Since Aum Shinrikyo was organized by the powerful leader, Shoko Asahara in 1984, he forcefully recruited them because he wanted their talents. From then on, they served under their leader and saw him as a God, breaking with their dear families and original lives. Ten members of this community were arrested with their boss as murderers in the sarin murder case. As a result, they were given the death penalty, except for Ikuo Hayashi, who delivered himself to the police and confessed his guilt. The members only acted according to their commander's selfish instructions because they could not oppose their awful leader. Indeed, they were also haunted by a fear that if they would not obey their leader's compulsory plan, they could be killed by other followers who would be ordered by their devilish chief. Thus, they also became wretched victims deprived of their precious lives.

*effect*

The most serious influence was that the sarin gas attack by Aum Shinrikyo led to some severe aftereffects in Japan. For example, a lot of people felt nervous about taking crowded trains or even being in public areas such as concert halls that were filled with a large audience; firework places, which should be enjoyable; and rest rooms in stations and parks. Also, the Japanese government removed all public trash cans in order to lessen people's fears. Even a small plastic bag became a source of anxiety for people. Trash cans in public places that should have been useful looked evil. Moreover, not only powerless citizens but also the police and mass communications became very sensitive to wherever people assembled. All mass media treated the tragedy and its aftermath as a lead story every day. In order to attract public interest, they frequently broadcast television programs about Aum Shinrikyo and got high ratings every time. It was an abnormal phenomenon. The more people got new facts from the shows, the more people became doubtful. Furthermore, people began to fear other Japanese religious fraternities, especially Soka Gakkai, which was similar to Aum Shinrikyo. Soka Gakkai had also gathered worldwide members and an extraordinary amount of their money, whose use was unknown. Although the members tried to calm people's suspicion, many people who did not belong to any religion became prejudiced against all religions. Therefore, the reputation of other innocent religious groups also was ironically damaged.

Who could expect that normal businessmen or students would be endangered by a poison like a lethal weapon at weekday rush hour on routine trains? Ordinarily, teenagers in Tokyo subways could relax enough to have a comfortable snooze with the soft sway of the trains or they might listen to their favorite music. Also, others might read their favorite books, daily newspapers, or popular magazines. However, the most serious attack in Japan since the end of the World War II cruelly and randomly took away their peaceful daily lives. It was completely impossible to imagine that a large invisible chemical could simultaneously be spread in subway trains while Japanese were going about their daily lives. This happened because Aum Shinrikyo recruited terrorists who caused heavy casualties and great national shock throughout Japan.

**Yoko Ohara**

# Problem/Solution Essay

A problem/solution essay presents a problem, usually discussing several aspects of the problem, then concludes by discussing solutions to the problem. The problem may be addressed in the following ways:

| | |
|---|---|
| 1. Effects only: | Describe the problem only in terms of its effects. Use examples. |
| 2. Causes and effects: | In addition to the effects, outline the causes of the problem. This approach is especially appropriate when discussing solutions in terms of preventive measures. |
| 3. Extended example: | After a topic sentence, illustrate the problem by using an extended example, e.g. tell the story of someone who experienced the problem, or continue the anecdote from your introduction. |

The solutions may be presented in various ways and you have to think about which way would be the most appropriate for the particular problem you are discussing. Here are some ways to present solutions:

| | |
|---|---|
| 1. Preventive measures: | Ways to prevent the problem from occurring in the first place, such as how to prevent skin cancer. |
| 2. A series of steps: | Suggest the easiest and most obvious solution first, but if that doesn't work, try something else, etc. For example, if you have a noisy neighbor, you might first talk to him/her; if that doesn't work, arrange for a mediator; etc. (a last resort might be to call the police). |
| 3. Advice: | Give some advice and helpful hints. |
| 4. A choice of solutions: | These solutions may be ones that have already been tried, including those which have been unsuccessful, and new solutions which you are proposing. |

Make sure that your essay is well-balanced. The most original part of your essay, and the section which will require the most critical thinking, will be the solutions. Make sure that you address the solutions in depth. The solutions section of the essay should be as long or longer than the section describing the problem.

**Suggestions for topics:**

Getting a baby to sleep
Preventing a burglary of your house or apartment
Dealing with stress
Raising children and working/taking classes
Rationing TV time for your children
Communicating effectively with your husband/wife/boss
Dealing with unwanted advances by a man/woman
Making friends with Americans
Making time for yourself
Dealing with a noisy neighbor
Caring for an elderly relative
Using a credit card wisely
Improving your G.P.A.
Raising a child as a single parent
Preventing teenage boys from joining gangs
Dealing with E-mail spam
Controlling the amount of e-mail you get
Restricting the Internet use of teenagers
Getting rid of your old appliances/computers
Keeping your house/apartment clean and tidy
Preventing pipes from freezing in the winter
Giving your children "quality time"
Making sure that household members share chores equally
Controlling dogs in your neighborhood
Controlling speeding drivers in the suburbs
Dealing with raccoons
Managing the stress of divorce
Coping with a heat wave
Dealing with snow and ice
Trying to prevent vandalism
Finding ways to deal with co-workers you don't like
Finding a fresh start after getting laid off
Dealing with telephone solicitations
Coping with a death in the family
Working on pronouncing English intelligibly
Dealing with relatives or friends who ask you for "favors" or money
Breaking up with a girlfriend/boyfriend

Your instructor may ask you to write a problem/solution essay related to just one topic, such as:

**education**          **your personal life**          **the environment**
**issues at your college/university**          **issues related to your own country**

Name: _____

## Problem/Solution Essay:  Peer Review

(You may use this exercise to review your own essay, one of your classmate's essays or one of the essays on pp. 71 - 74)

Title: _____

Writer: _____

1.   Write the thesis statement below.

2.   Does the thesis statement mention the topic, the focus of the essay, and the idea that the author will address solutions?

3.   Does the writer begin the essay with an interesting anecdote or explanation? What is it about?

4.   Is the essay well-balanced? Is there sufficient attention given to both the problem and possible solutions?

5.   Is the conclusion effective?  If not, how would you change it?

6.   In your opinion, what is the best part of this essay, and why?

7.  Which part of this essay is the least effective?  How would you suggest that the writer change it?

8.  Write a paragraph in response to your classmate's essay.

## Problem/Solution Essay: Example #1

### Don't Be a Target

"This is just like I have got an ATM in my room!" When I used Internet Banking at first, I was impressed by the usefulness of the Online Banking system. Thanks to the Internet, rapid information technology advances have led us to a more convenient world. Now we can manage our own account without going to the bank. Even if you don't have enough time to go to a bank, you will immediately be able to transfer your money by using the Internet. However, in this convenient way to access a bank account, your money might be exposed to serious problems and has the potential to be stolen by someone whom you don't know. To protect our property from crime, and to use the Internet Banking effectively, there are several ways in which we should pay more careful attention.

A few years ago, my sister told me that, on her credit history, she had found some weird withdrawals. According to my sister, one day she was looking at her credit account to check monthly payments by using the Internet. Actually, she hadn't recognized the fact, until that day, that a small amount of money had been taken from her account over a few months. She wondered what she had paid for, so she soon checked all receipts, which she had kept just in case. However, she couldn't find any receipts for the payments. Moreover, she still had no idea about the purchases, so she called to the bank and asked a bank worker to stop the account. Fortunately, the bank returned the money to her, and the bank worker said to her she might have been cheated on her credit number and password while she was shopping online.

If so, how can we protect money from crime? First, the most basic thing is don't access your bank account from the computers in an Internet cafe or other public places. The computers in public places have a much greater possibility to be a target of the "Key Logger" program. If the program is set up on a computer, the program will memorize every key operation which you type. Furthermore, the program has an automatic function itself to send the collected information, such as your password or ID number, to the criminal.

Next, you shouldn't keep the same password for a long time. Even if you only accessed the bank account from your own computer, it's not enough to prevent your account being a target. Especially, if you are using the automatic login system, the possibility to be cheated on your password will increase. Hackers have attempted various ways to get people's information; furthermore, hacking is not such a difficult thing to do. Therefore, we have to recognize that our security isn't perfect any time and we should make a new password frequently.

Another way to protect your account is to avoid using your password for just any request. Recently, many people have been damaged by ".phishing." The technique to steal people's account information is simple but intricate. The criminal sends an HTML e-mail which pretends it comes from the bank. The form looks just like a real web site, so customers put their information in the fake window without deep concern.

In addition to these ways, we shouldn't forget to check our own account history regularly. And then, if you find a strange record, you should immediately call the customer service center of the bank. If you find it sooner, the bank's response will be better, and your lost money will be recovered.

As online banking becomes popular, many problems can potentially result. Sometimes we have an unexpected and serious problem. To make good use of the online systems, we have to take appropriate steps and have to protect own property from `high–tech" crimes. Sometimes, Internet banking is really useful for us; however, we might lose financial security if we're not careful.

**Mayumi Mori**

# Problem/Solution Essay: Example #2

## Sense of Place

"Why did I come here?" This is a question that I have asked myself many times since my family immigrated to America. I was so depressed and frustrated that I really wanted to go back to China after a short period of time. In my mind, I kept thinking that this was not my home. I didn't know how to settle down in this new country. What's more, not only me, but also my parents had the same feeling. Therefore, my family has experienced culture shock. Culture shock is an unavoidable problem that many people need to face and solve when they go to a new country.

As Dr. Carmen Guanipa of San Diego State University, states, "The term, culture shock . . . expresses the lack of direction, the feeling of not knowing what to do or how to do things in a new environment, and not knowing what is appropriate or inappropriate." Since different countries have different cultures, when people get into a new country, they may encounter different challenges. Because people have different views about beliefs, values, and norms, it is not easy to adjust to a new culture. They can't live in the same way as they did before. Therefore, they will feel strange when they meet situations which are unfamiliar to them, and they don't know how to solve their problems properly. For example, after I came to America, the first big challenge that I encountered was the language. Although I had learned some English before I came here, that was far from enough. Having problems in communicating with other people often makes me worried. When I need to go to study in college, I'm always afraid that I can't understand the courses because college is difficult. Before people come to a new country, they may be excited and enthusiastic. However, when they come to the new country, after short term of being excited, they will encounter difficulties instead of interesting experiences. When people suffer from culture shock, they may feel sad, lonely, dejected and stressed. They may not sleep well. They don't have confidence to do things. These can cause people to have bad health. Consequently, people should take the problem of culture shock seriously and find ways to overcome it.

The first way that people can try is changing their attitude. When people have culture shock, they don't feel comfortable in the new place. They may think the new environment won't accept them, so they don't adjust to the new environment. They may only see the negative side of things. People should try to think about all the things positively. Culture shock can provide a chance for people to redefine their life objectives, though it can make people feel real pain. People can take this great chance to learn and obtain new perspectives. According to Dr. Guanipa, culture shock can let people know more about themselves and activate their creativity. When people can deal with their negative feelings, it's easier to develop a new comprehension of the things that they don't understand. They can try to figure out a suitable way to live in the new place. I try this way when I am affected by culture shock. I tell myself that since I came here, I should accept all the difficulties, though it takes time to overcome them. Actually, I find that living in a new country not only gives me a new look at life, but also trains my own abilities. A good attitude can help people get through culture shock more easily.

Another way that people can try is to force themselves out into the new environment. Some people don't like to communicate with native speakers or join their activities. They only like to stay at home. It is not a good way to know more about the new culture. Some people like to read the newspaper or watch TV in order to know more about the new place. However, talking with the native speakers is more efficient. People not only can practice the language, but also can know more things about the new place. Through different conversations or activities, people may find some new things which they are interested in about the new place. That is one way that can help people kill their loneliness. For example, I have a friend who is an international student. At first, she was afraid of talking with people because she thought her English was bad and didn't know what kind of topics she should talk about. Even when she was with her host family, she preferred to stay in her own room. Gradually, she found that she was so lonely, and she still knew nothing about the new place. She tried to force herself to communicate with people, and her host family helped her to know more about the new culture. Now, she feels more comfortable in this new place. When people can put themselves into a new culture, they can enjoy the new culture more.

Culture shock commonly happens to people who have to live in a new country. It can have a negative effect on people. Therefore, people should take some positive steps such as changing their attitude and putting themselves into the new environment in order to solve this problem. If people have patience to go through the difficulty of culture shock, they can learn how to interact with a different culture and find that it's a valuable experience for their life.

**Jieyi Peng**

# Argument Essay

An argument essay explores a controversial issue, one where various opinions may differ. In addition to describing the issue, you must try to get the reader to accept your point of view. You can do this by offering logical proof in a reasonable way. A good argument offers facts, examples, details, or statistics. These should either be well-known, or come from an authority on the topic. In some cases, you might support your argument with interviews. An argument involves critical thinking. Avoid fallacies and propaganda. Critical thinkers are well-informed about both sides of an issue. They can understand weaknesses in their own and their opponents' arguments and can also recognize points of compromise.

---

### Organization

1.  Illustrate the issue using an anecdote, explanation, etc.; briefly explain both sides of the argument; include a thesis statement showing your position.

2.  Develop the argument by discussing and using verifiable evidence (use several paragraphs here).

3.  Mention and refute counter arguments to the points you have discussed.

4.  Reexamine your position and reevaluate its correctness. End with a warning, prediction, or value judgment.

**Note:** It could be more useful to put the refutation <u>before</u> the paragraphs where you express your own point-of-view. Another organizational pattern in the body of the essay would be to use your own arguments to refute each of the opponents' arguments (point-counter-point). See p. 68 - 69.

---

## Making a good argument

When writing an argument paper, some types of argument are more appropriate than others. For example, an argument needs to be free of bias, vagueness, and over-reliance on personal beliefs. In order to make your argument appealing and credible, use the following methods:

1.  Opinions of experts: using the words of well-known experts to support your views
2.  Supported generalization: using facts, figures, and case studies to support a general statement.
3.  Personal experience: relate the argument to your own experience or the experiences of people that you know.
4.  Solid research and documentation from a variety of sources (different periodicals, interviews, etc.)
5.  Careful refutation of the opponents' arguments, showing a balanced and fair consideration, not bias.

**Examples of poor arguments:**

1. Generalization: stating that "everyone" thinks a certain way, or that "people" do things a certain way, e.g. "All Americans watch too much T.V." Be more specific!

2. Stereotype: for example, "All Americans are loud and rude"; "(certain nationalities) are lazy."

3. Threat: warning your audience of drastic consequences, e.g. "We will all be dead in 50 years if we don't take care of the ozone problem now."

4. Distortion: twisting arguments of your opponents in order to make your own argument stronger, e.g. "Pro-Choice supporters are really pro-death because they believe in abortion."

5. Slander: trying to persuade through emotional or false statement rather than reason, e.g. "High school teachers get paid too much money and they they don't deserve it because they are so lazy."

6. Religious belief: using your religious convictions as proof. Not everyone will have the same beliefs as you do, and you need to convince a wider audience.

7. Poor reasoning: drawing conclusions that are not necessarily true or may be based on incomplete evidence, e.g. "After interviewing two Americans who were opposed to capital punishment, I can see most Americans are opposed to capital punishment."

Note:

Emotions tend to distort arguments and make your position unattractive to the reader. Good arguments should be based upon facts, not feelings. Try to avoid topics that you have very strong feelings about. Your feelings may show you to be too biased. Instead, choose a topic that you can study dispassionately. Then you should be able to analyze all sides of the controversy reasonably

## Refuting opposing arguments

In an essay where you give the opponents' arguments after you make your own arguments, you should give one or two of the opponents' strongest points. Usually, these points will focus on <u>different aspects of the issue</u> than the ones you have already given. When you <u>refute</u> the opponents' arguments, you don't have to prove that they are wrong. You can suggest that the arguments that they are focusing on are not as important as the arguments that you have raised, or you can allow some <u>concessions</u> and suggest some <u>compromises</u> that would still allow your case to be the stronger of the two.

The following is a sample outline of the pros and cons in an argument:

---

Topic: "Eating and drinking should be allowed in the class."

Pros:  1. Some students don't have time to eat outside of class;

2. It allows for a more relaxed atmosphere, which helps students to learn;

3. It's a matter of individual freedom: allow eating and drinking as long as it doesn't interfere with the class.

Cons:  1. It can be messy; students in a following class may sit on some Coke that has been spilled on a seat, and the janitors complain about having to clean up too many spills.

Refutation:  The janitors are paid to clean the classrooms; Messy students can be fined, or they can be told to clean up their own messes; most students are not messy.

2. It can be noisy: for example, someone eating potato chips; the the smell of food can also be distracting to other students.

Refutation:  Most foods do not have strong smells; noisy eaters can be asked to stop, just like noisy talkers.

---

You will notice that the arguments *pro* focus on different aspects of the issue than the arguments *con*. The arguments *pro* need to be developed with strong, authoritative evidence and examples; you may make some concessions when you refute the arguments *con*, but don't make these arguments seem more attractive than your own.

# Argument vocabulary

## People:

| | |
|---|---|
| proponents | opponents |
| supporters | detractors |
| defenders | |
| advocates | |
| pro- | anti- |

## Verbs:

| | | | |
|---|---|---|---|
| believe | theorize | acknowledge | recognize |
| contend | fear | concede | realize |
| argue | estimate | admit | counter |
| claim | project | grant | disprove |
| assert | accept | rebut | advocate |
| refute | favor (be in favor of) | | |

## Nouns:

belief
contention
claim
argument
conclusion
assertion

## Adjectives:

inaccurate
incomplete
(in)valid
illogical
unproved

## Transitions:

however
on the contrary (meaning: that isn't true)
conversely
on the other hand
despite this (fact)
in spite of (this)
although
while
actually
furthermore
in addition
nevertheless
therefore
thus

## Controversial issues to write about

Choose your topic very carefully. If you can find a subject that is interesting for you, you will enjoy writing your essay more and probably do a better job. Make sure that your topic isn't too broad. Your arguments should be comprehensive. Choosing a manageable topic will make it possible to stay within the three to five page range while still effectively presenting all the arguments necessary to persuade the reader. You instructor may also require you to write about a certain topic or give you a choice of topics.

You could also argue a social or political situation in your country if you are able to obtain the necessary factual information. Some topics in the news include the following:

| | | |
|---|---|---|
| farming animals for their fur | Internet censorship | genetic engineering |
| food labels | legalized gambling | term limits for politicians |
| jail reform | cell phones/driving | trade policies |
| giving money to panhandlers | English Only laws | legalized prostitution |
| home schooling | tax reform | mandatory retirement |
| birth control policies | recycling | protection of old growth forests |
| the Internet in education | school budgets | curfews for teenagers |
| MySpace.com | bilingual education | raising the minimum wage |
| protecting the salmon | landmines | U.N. sanctions and embargoes |
| price of college textbooks | politicians' sex lives | U.S. immigration policy |
| manned mission to Mars | medical marijuana | raising the driving age |
| spanking children | distance learning | drilling for oil in the Arctic |

## Other topics:

Having a baby after the traditional childbearing years
Returning to one's native country to find a marriage partner
Requiring foreign language proficiency for high school graduation in Oregon
Having women serve in combat in the military
Providing nursing home care for an elderly relative
Requiring welfare recipients to work while receiving benefits
Placing prisons in population centers
Allowing sex offenders to return to their communities without warning neighbors
Providing educational and medical services to illegal immigrants
Teaching pre-school children two languages
Requiring engaged couples to have counseling before marriage
Reducing the future number of legal immigrants permitted to enter the U.S
Using animals in laboratory experiments
Rating video games more strictly
Using photo radar at traffic lights

Of course, it is always a wise choice to pick an issue with which you have had some experience, such as education, parenting, neighborhood issues, or a controversial topic from your own country. Otherwise, you may have to do some time-consuming research to familiarize yourself with the topic.

In addition, it is always important to **narrow your topic**. After choosing an issue, try to confine your opinions about it to a particular place, time, or country. Make sure that this is clear in your thesis statement.

**Some advice:**

The following topics have been written about so much that all of the arguments on both sides are already familiar to most readers. Please choose a topic that is not related to these subjects:

| | |
|---|---|
| abortion | capital punishment/the death penalty |
| euthanasia/assisted suicide | working mothers |
| smoking | alcohol/drinking and driving |
| gun control | sex and violence on TV |
| human cloning | gay marriage |

**Sample student thesis statements:**

The following are examples of thesis statements from student essays:

It should be legal for married couples in Japan to have different surnames.
The practice of bride price among the Kikuyu is often punitive and prices should be lowered to a token amount.
Adoptees should have the right to know the identities of their birth parents when they become teenagers.
The U.S. Embassy in Vietnam should re-issue F1 visas for students more easily.
Burundi's Tutsi-dominated army should integrate members of the majority Hutu into its ranks.
Because college textbooks have become so expensive, we need to regulate publishers' practices.
Marijuana should be legally marketed as a source of fuel and fiber.
There should be stricter controls over liposuction.
Google should resist the Government's subpoena to submit user records in the name of the Child Online Protection Act.
Prime Minister Koizumi of Japan should cease his visits to Yasukuni Shrine in honor of war veterans.
Montessori schools are an excellent choice for parents seeking an alternative kind of education for their children.
The United States should drill for oil in the Arctic National Wildlife Refuge.
Miyagi Prefecture should continue with its system of single-sex high schools.
The government of Thailand needs to crack down on the use of amphetamines in night clubs.
English immersion, rather than bilingual education, should be the program of choice for ESL students in public elementary schools.
The United States government should require labeling of all foods derived from GMOs (genetically modified organisms).
Cat owners should have their pets neutered to prevent unwanted problems.

Exercise 12

**Practice arguments for debate**

After you choose your topic, it would be a good idea to debate the issue with a classmate or friend. This way, you can discover some of the objections to your point-of-view.

The following arguments fall under the general topic of "education". Find a group of three to five other people and divide the group in half. Choose one of the topics below and stage an informal debate. One half of the group will support the statement and the other half will oppose it. (It doesn't matter what your personal beliefs are: you must be able to argue for either viewpoint). Your debate will consist of arguments and counter-arguments (refutations).

1. High schools should be segregated by sex.

2. Smoking should not be allowed anywhere on the college campus.

3. The current grading system (A-F) should be eliminated in favor of no grades, just C (completed) or I (incomplete).

4. People should pay higher taxes to maintain quality in public schools.

5. Class size at a college should be kept at 15 students or fewer.

6. Attendance should not be part of the final grade in a college course.

7. An instructor's salary should depend upon the students' evaluation of his/her performance.

8. American high school students should wear uniforms.

9. American schools should begin the instruction of foreign languages at the elementary school level.

10. All college students should be required to take a P.E. class every term.

# Organization plans for an argument essay

There are different ways to organize an argument essay. Your selection will depend on your topic and what you intend to emphasize. See the two plans below. Note that the number of paragraphs is up to you.

## Plan 1

1.  Introduction (attention-getting material)

    Thesis statement:

    _____ should _____ because _____

2.  Opponents argument #1  +  your refutation

3.  Opponents argument #2  +  your refutation

4.  Opponents argument #3  +  your refutation

5.  Opponents argument #4  +  your refutation

6.  Opponents argument #5  +  your refutation

| support paragraphs with details, examples and personal experience |
| --- |

7.  Conclusion

## Plan 2

1.  Introduction (attention-getting material)

    Thesis statement:

    _____ should _____ because _____

2.  Opponents argument #1  +  your refutation

3.  Opponents argument #2  +  your refutation

4.  Opponents argument #3  +  your refutation

| support paragraphs with details, examples and personal experience |
| --- |

5.  Your argument #1

6.  Your argument #2

7.  Your argument #3

8.  Your argument #4

9.  Your argument #5

10. Conclusion

Name: _____

**Peer Review: Argument Essay**
(You may use this exercise to review your own essay, one of your classmate's essays or the essays on pp. 85-88 and p. 145)

Title: _____

Writer: _____

1.     Write the thesis statement of the essay.

2.     What kind of introduction does it have (anecdote, statistics, statement by expert, etc.?)

3.     Is the introduction interesting and effective? Why/why not?

4.     How many different arguments does the author make?

List the arguments below:

5.     List the opponents' arguments that the author gives.

6.     Are the refutations effective?  Why/Why not?

7.      Is the conclusion effective?  Why / Why not?

8.      What is the best part of the essay?  Why?

9.      What is the least effective part of the essay?  Give a suggestion on how the writer could improve it.

10.     Write a short paragraph in response to your classmate's essay.

# Argument Essay: Example #1

(see also the example at the end of the *Handbook*)

## Save the Planet

As if it were not confusing enough for us to read the nutrition labels at the grocery stores, we have to think what the best answer is to the most popular question at the cashier "Paper or plastic?" when we try to do our best for the planet. For the last few years, the global climate has being changing drastically, and it seems like our everyday lifestyle and needs are a big contribution to the devastating effects on our planet. Among so many other factors, the so common paper and plastic grocery bags we use also have a big impact on the environment and the statistics on which one is better can be quite confusing. I have been just as confused as most people probably are about "Paper vs. plastic;" in fact, even before reading some of the statistics, I was inclined to use paper most of the time, but now I know that by choosing paper bags at the grocery store from the first use, to the reuse and the recycle, we can take a better approach to having a cleaner planet.

*Concession* ○ Many statistics show that plastic bags are by far less expensive to make than paper bags being made from petroleum. This is the reason why, "In 1980, many supermarkets switched from using paper bags to plastic since the plastic (polyethylene) bags are less expensive" (Brower & Leon); in addition, plastic bags are weightless and have smaller volume so less fuel is needed to ship them around.

People may say that grocery paper bags cost more than plastic bags when making new ones, but they have a higher rate of recycling and the cost of making a new paper bag from a recycled one brings paper bags to a lower use of energy; in short, the recycling rate of paper bags brings the cost down. Another advantage is that "paper bags are made from renewable material – wood" (Milstein). Also petroleum, which is used to make plastic bags, is a nonrenewable resource, and it is not cheap anymore; it is also another question how long the resources of oil are going to last. In addition, as the owner of Far West Fibers mentions, because of plastic bags mixed with other recycling materials, sorting crews have to spend thirty percent of their time cleaning the sorting machines from the tangled plastic bags that are in people's recycling bins (Milstein). For many people it is much harder to recycle plastic bags since there are very few places that take them back

Some times plastic bags are more convenient because it seems that the handles are stronger than paper bags; also, they protect your merchandise and don't break in the rain, and if the eggs break you have less chance of getting your car dirty if the bag was tied well. On the other hand, if we use paper bags at the grocery store we need much fewer than plastic bags because you can fit about four times more into a paper bag then a plastic bag. Besides the rate of reusing paper bags is high since many stores reimburse customers if they bring their own bags. Another way we can reuse paper bags at home is to store things in them. They look nice, last forever on the storage shelves, and hold a lot more than plastic bags.

When it comes to air and water pollution, we may think we have got a winner by choosing plastic bags because many statistics show that less water and less air is polluted in the process of making plastic bags. However, it is impossible not to notice plastic bags flying in the air even under the smallest wind causing other types of pollution. It is not only unaesthetic to see trees decorated with the flying bags, but it is dangerous for the animals and birds that get caught inside the bags (Haberman). If paper bags are not recycled and they go with the regular garbage, it is not as bad as throwing away plastic bags because paper is biodegradable and it decomposes faster than plastic, which is a plus for the environment knowing how many years it takes for plastic to decompose.

While paper bags have higher recycle rate, it is less likely we will see them flying in the air or strangling small animals. That makes paper bags less of a hazard to wildlife and helps to keep the environment cleaner; this is a big factor why countries like South Africa and Taiwan banned the use of plastic bags and also San Francisco adopted the same measure (McKinley).

Despite the fact, that paper bags and plastic bags have pros and cons, we have to make the best decision on using, reusing, and recycling to improve the climate on our planet because both use natural resources and are big contributors to pollution ("Paper Bags Are Better Than Plastic, Right?"). We have to use, reuse and recycle our resources carefully and perhaps next time when we go to the grocery we can bring along some paper bags from home and then we know for sure that's a plus for the environment.

## Works Cited

Brower, Michael and Leon, Warren. "Paper or Plastic?" *Grassroots Recycling Network.*
    22 May 2007 < http://www.grrn.org/resources/paper_plastic.html>
Haberman, Clyde. "In Winter, Trees Bear Plastic Fruit." *The New York Times,*
    6 Feb 2004, late ed.: B1. ProQuest. Portland Community College Library,
    Portland, OR. 28 May 2007.
McKinley, Jesse. "San Francisco Board Votes to Ban Some Plastic Bags."
    *The New York Times* 28 March 2007, late ed.: A16. ProQuest
    Portland Community College Library, Portland, OR. 28 May 2007
Milstein, Michael. "Paper or Plastic?" *The Oregonian,* May 17th 2007. A1, A13.
"Paper Bags Are Better Than Plastic, Right?" 2007. Reusable Bags.com.  22 May 2007
    < http://www.reusablebags.com/>

**Dorina Shari**

# Argument Essay: Example #2

(see also the example at the end of the *Handbook*)

## Keep Your Hands to Yourself!

I didn't know an "International Spank Out Day", which is on April 30th, has existed since 1998 until I recently found it on the Internet. This day was designated because its supporters hope that it will raise awareness about the dangers of corporal punishment such as spanking. Unfortunately, I also found a piece of news which reported that a spanked woman compared her punishment to rape. In *Spanking Harms Children, Especially Girls,* Melinda Rice described the experience of a female student in a Florida high school, was paddled by a male administrator. She was being made to bend over his desk and stretch out her legs while she was wearing a mini skirt. At this time, another male administrator was attracted by this scene. The first male administrator struck her hard three times. The woman never told this to anybody until she wrote the letter. In the woman's words, it was the closest thing to a rape as she could imagine. I am wondering whether it would have evolved into rape if there had been nobody around him. Nowadays, there are still some people who contend that spanking children is a good way to teach them. However, spanking is harmful for children's health, hearts and minds.

Children will behave well if parents have more patience. I had an experience when I went to a library one day in China. I was attracted by some noise, and then I turned my head and saw a young mother was arguing with her little daughter. It seemed that the mother wanted to finish her book before she left, but the little girl refused to read her books. The young mother became weary, and said loudly, "Just go to read the books you like. I have already told you that we will not leave until I finish the book." However, the little girl shook her head. At this time, her mother slapped her daughter's face sharply, and then everyone in library was shocked. With little girl's crying, her mother felt guilty and said, "Go read your books, okay?" The little girl still stood there. The young mother was embarrassed and asked her daughter that if she wanted to sit next to her and waited until she finished the book. The girl nodded her head. In this case, the little girl just wanted to stay with her mother. People sometimes think that children are being unreasonable and hard to communicate with if they are insubordinate. In fact, children are innocent and naïve and if parents have more patience, it is not hard to communicate with their children.

Spanking children is not a good long-term way to teach them. Actually, "Spanking a child will stop the child from misbehaving for the moment, but studies have shown that the child's compliance will only last for a short time; corporal punishment actually increases the child's non-compliant behavior in the future" (*"Child corporal punishment: spanking"*). Children just have to face what their parents do, but deep inside they believe that they are innocent, and it was not their fault. Punishment might even make children hate their parents. For instance, one of my cousins ShanXin, who is in China, is outgoing but audacious and hard to control. Moreover, she always got "Fs" in her classes. As a result of that, scolding and spanking became a normal part of ShanXin and her mother's daily lives. I still remember that once I asked ShanXin if she understood why her mother spanked and scolded her. She answered secretly that she didn't agree with her mother's words and didn't think she had done something wrong. Spanking her made her behave worse because she wanted to get revenge on her mother. She pretended to behave well in front of her mother, and she said sorry immediately if she found her mother was trying to slap her. However, when she was behind her mother's back, she was naughty again. She told me that she didn't like her mother anymore. Through her words, I felt that she thought she was being smart by behaving worse behind her mother's back in order to pay back her mom. However, she didn't think she was wrong. This case shows that it is not necessary to spank a child.

However, the opponents contend that corporal punishment is a normal disciplinary way to raise children. They consider that spanking and yelling at children to discipline them and teach them what is good and what is bad, is for their own good. My grandmother, JieQing Huang, whom I interviewed on May 31, 2007, said, "Spanking was not bad for me, and I am so good right now. I claim that children would not behave well if parents do not spank them. Once children feel painful after being spanked, they notice that they did something wrong. Then they will remember and be afraid to do it again." My dad was raised by my grandmother. She spanked my dad when he was naughty and refused to study. In her opinion, punishment is necessary for parents to raise their children. Furthermore, the excessive doting on children without punishment could lead to destroy the youths' lives. She believes that children should be praised when their behavior is well; they should be punished when they behave badly. Today she usually praises me and gives a small present if I behave well. She asserted that although more and more abandonment of corporal punishment are permitted today, she believes that punishment is a helpful way to bring up children. However, she doesn't know that spanking my dad left him was a bad experience which made him introverted and not easy to get along with now.

In conclusion, different people use different methods to raise their children. However, I prefer raising children without corporal punishment. Because raising children without spanking would make children healthy, parents should teach their children without violence. In order to love children and make them happy, parents should have more patience for them and care about their thoughts more.

## Works Cited

Robinson, B.A. "Child Corporal Punishment: Spanking". *Religious Tolerance.* 2007.
    Ontario Consultants on Religious Tolerance. 1 June, 2007
    <http://www.religioustolerance.org/spankin3.htm>.
Rice, Melinda. "Experts: Spanking Harms Children, Especially Girls". *Women's eNews.*
    2007. June 6, 2007 < http://www.womensenews.org/article.cfm/
    dyn/aid/662/context/archive>.
"Spank Out Day". *Canadian Children's Rights Council.* 2007. Canadian Children's Rights
    Council. June 1, 2007 <http://www.canadiancrc.com/SpankOut_Day_April_30th.htm>.

**Xi Zhong**

Exercise 13

Six basic rhetorical (organizational) styles have been addressed in this handbook: Description, Classification, Definition, Cause/Effect, Problem/Solution, and Argument.

Imagine that you want to write essays using the topics below. Think about how you would develop the topics and choose a rhetorical style that is appropriate to each topic.

To the left of each topic, write one of the following:

| | |
|---|---|
| **DES** | (Description) |
| **CL** | (Classification) |
| **DEF** | (Definition) |
| **CE** | (Cause/Effect) |
| **PS** | (Problem/Solution) |
| **ARG** | (Argument). |

_____ 1. An opinion that law enforcement officials should be permitted to access MySpace.com sites in order to track sexual predators.

_____ 2. An in-depth exploration of the meaning of the word "patriotism"

_____ 3. Why people get culture shock and how they can overcome it

_____ 4. A visually stimulating experience while traveling in another country

_____ 5. What happens when teenagers spend too much time on their Xbox or GameCube

_____ 6. A breakdown of three different types of sports fans at a soccer match

_____ 7. An explanation of a word from your native language that doesn't translate well into English

_____ 8. Resolving a serious marital problem

_____ 9. Making a strong case for raising a child bilingually

_____ 10. An explanation of different styles of basketball play

_____ 11. Why some people like to go skydiving

_____ 12. A detailed description of your wedding day

# IN-CLASS WRITING

## Purpose of In-class Writing

The purpose of in-class writing is to test the student's real writing ability under examination conditions. Students will not know the essay questions before the in-class test. They should apply all they have learned in terms of essay development, organization, the thesis statement, syntax, and grammar. In the evaluation of in-class writing, instructors pay a lot of attention to correct sentence structure. Students who are still making grammatical errors in every sentence will probably not pass an in-class writing test.

In-class essays are hand-written on lined paper unless the class is asked to write in a computer lab. You should write double-spaced - this makes it easier for the instructor to read and comment on your writing. You will usually be given a certain amount of time, such as 60 minutes, to complete an in-class essay test. You should not be allowed to continue writing after the class period has ended.

Some students get very nervous during in-class writing tests. Ideas seem to vanish as soon as they get in the classroom, and they forget simple grammar rules. They are not alone! If you get nervous, use your time wisely at the beginning of the period. Write down your ideas in an organized outline. If you have a choice of topics, pay special attention to topic selection. Choose a topic which you can easily write about without stopping too long. Focus on the organization of your essay and your basic sentence structure. Most instructors will not allow you to bring notes in to your in-class writing test.

## Preparation

Here are some suggestions for an in-class writing assignment that takes one hour.

1.      Spend at least 10 minutes at the beginning writing an outline of the following: a clear introduction with thesis statement; topic sentences and examples for a limited number of body paragraphs; a brief conclusion. See the sample essay outline on page 4.

2.      Spend about 35 - 40 minutes writing the essay. Don't write too much: the basic requirements for a good in-class essay will be logical development of ideas, clear organization, and sound sentence structure and punctuation.

3.      Revise and edit for the final 10 - 15 minutes of class. Review for errors in usage of articles, verb tenses, verb forms, subject-verb agreement, prepositions, noun plurals, word forms, vocabulary, punctuation, and spelling. You may even have time to rewrite parts of the essay.

Remember that the body paragraphs of your in-class essay should form the bulk of your writing. These should contain interesting details, explanations, and examples to illustrate your topic sentence. It is not the number of paragraphs, but rather how well they are developed which is important.

# Reading Response

Some writing assignments, including in-class writing assignments, may require you to 'respond' to an assigned reading. Of course, you will need to spend some time reading the assignment and making sure that you understand it fully before you respond to it. The most important part of the reading response is your thesis statement, in which you have to present an original idea based on the ideas in the reading.

Instructors may give you a question, or a set of questions to choose from, based on the reading. You will not know these questions before you take an in-class writing test. Make sure that your thesis statement conforms to the question that you have chosen to answer.

An essay question based on a reading may take one of the following forms, or a combination thereof:

| | |
|---|---|
| a. | disagreement with the author point by point |
| b. | agreement with the author point by point |
| c. | pros and cons of the issue (discussion) |
| d. | your views on the issue (argument) |
| e. | comparison or contrast with a similar situation |
| f. | relationship of the issue to your own experience |
| g. | expansion of the topic to include your own details and examples |
| h. | an extended example of someone or something influenced by the issue |

A reading response can be based on the following outline:

Part 1:      a. **Summary** of the author's main idea(s) <u>in your own words</u>.
             Use two to five sentences. Be brief!

             See the section on short summaries, pages 121 – 126.

             Your first sentence should mention the author's name, the title of the
             article and give the **main idea** of the reading.

          b. **Thesis statement** (<u>your</u> main idea). Use one sentence. You will
             probably have to use a **transition sentence** between the summary
             of the article and the thesis statement.

             See the examples of introductory paragraphs on the next page and
             for the reading response essay example on pages 95 - 96.

Part 2:      Respond to the article in your own words. Each paragraph should
             have a **topic sentence**. Use **transition words**. This will be the
             lengthiest part of your essay. You have already briefly summarized
             the article, so don't repeat ideas from the reading in detail. In this
             part of the essay, you should be focusing on your own ideas and
             supporting your thesis statement. Use **interesting details** and **specific
             examples**.

Part 3:      A brief conclusion in which you **synthesize** the points made by the
             author of the reading and your own ideas.

**Examples of introductory paragraphs for a reading response essay**

Below are some essay questions for an article entitled "Sexism in the Schoolhouse" (The article is not in this handbook).

1.  **Do you agree with the report of the American Association of University Women that boys and girls are not treated equally in the U.S. school system? Write an essay which includes your own personal observations on this issue. You may refer to the article in your essay.**

2.  **Are boys and girls treated equally in the school system in your country? You may want to focus your essay on one particular aspect of this topic, for example universities or elementary schools. Give examples from your own experience if you can.**

Here are some examples of introductory paragraphs in answer to the questions above. Note that each question can be answered in different ways. The summaries in the paragraphs below are the same, but the transition sentences or words and the thesis statements (underlined) are different. There is also the beginning of a body paragraph for each essay.

**In answer to question 1:**

Barbara Kantrowitz, in "Sexism in the Schoolhouse," outlines a study by the American Association of University Women which asserts that the U.S. school system favors boys over girls. The study lists several reasons for this problem. The effect is that girls often have less confidence in their abilities and are not as ambitious as boys. Kantrowitz mentions some solutions by education experts. <u>However, the school system in the U.S. does treat boys and girls fairly</u>.

In high school classes, both boys and girls are called on by the teacher. For example, when I was at Madison High . . .

---

Barbara Kantrowitz, in "Sexism in the Schoolhouse," outlines a study by the American Association of University Women which asserts that the U.S. school system favors boys over girls. The study lists several reasons for this problem. The effect is that girls often have less confidence in their abilities and are not as ambitious as boys. Kantrowitz mentions some solutions by education experts. The article supports my own experience. <u>The school system in the U.S. treats boys and girls unequally</u>.

In my daughter's elementary school, it is clear that the teachers allow boys to exhibit disruptive behavior when girls are reprimanded for the same behavior. For example, . . .

---

**In answer to question 2:**


Barbara Kantrowitz, in "Sexism in the Schoolhouse," outlines a study by the American Association of University Women which asserts that the U.S. school system favors boys over girls. The study lists several reasons for this problem. The effect is that girls often have less confidence in their abilities and are not as ambitious as boys. Kantrowitz mentions some solutions by education experts. A worse situation exists in some other countries. <u>The school system in Burkina Faso does not treat boys and girls equally at all</u>.

Teachers in Burkina Faso tend to ignore girls in the classroom. One reason for this is . . .

---

Barbara Kantrowitz, in "Sexism in the Schoolhouse," outlines a study by the American Association of University Women which asserts that the U.S. school system favors boys over girls. The study lists several reasons for this problem. The effect is that girls often have less confidence in their abilities and are not as ambitious as boys. Kantrowitz mentions some solutions by education experts. This situation does not exist in some other countries. <u>The school system in San Marino deals with boys and girls fairly in every respect.</u>

My instructors in San Marino felt that there was no typically "female" or "male" behavior. For example, Luigi, a male friend of mine, was quiet and shy in class. The teachers compensated for this by . . .

---

**Example of a reader response to "Are American Schools Too Easy?"** (pp. 104 - 105)

## A National Curriculum in Russia

In the article "Are American Schools Too Easy?", Albert Shanker states that students from countries with national curriculums are better educated than American students because they have more assignments and have to work harder to get them done. The author lists several negative points of the American educational system, such as very broadly defined curriculums, negotiable schoolwork, and varying amounts of schoolwork depending on teachers. He believes that a national curriculum can change this situation. My country, Russia, has a national curriculum. From my experience, there are both advantages and disadvantages to having a national curriculum.

Let's start with the positive points. First, because the educational system is the same for the whole country, there is no problem with moving from one city to another and changing schools. For example, my family traveled a lot, and I changed many schools and teachers. It did not matter what part of the country we were in, whether it was the middle of the term or the end, we studied the same subjects and read the same books, and the teachers' expectations were the same. Second, students and their parents, as well as teachers, know what is required. We had to study hard to get all our school assignments done. Nobody could even think about negotiating schoolwork. The third advantage of a national curriculum is that most of the students after graduation are better prepared for getting degrees in colleges or universities. The harder you study the better your knowledge is, and the better your chances are to attend college.

There are some disadvantages to a national curriculum. First, students do not have a choice. All subjects are required. When I was a student, I sometimes felt that I wasted my time studying subjects which were boring and useless for me instead of taking interesting classes. Later, I had to fight with my son's teacher and the school principal about taking English instead of German. In contrast, here in the U.S. for his next school year, my sixth grade son can choose subjects interesting to him from a bigger variety. He is so proud that he can decide for himself what to study. Second, bad grades in even one insignificant subject can hurt his chances of going to college. Is it vital for future programmers, teachers or artists to run fast and jump high? Yes, good health is important, but they are not going to be sportsmen and Olympic champions. Another negative point is that there is no special program for children with special needs. For example, a boy in my class whose family moved from West Ukraine failed Russian and had to stay in the same class for two years. We did not have teachers who taught Russian for non-native speakers.

Finally, our children spend almost all day in school, and I think it is very important how they feel, if they enjoy studying new things or they are bored, tired, or depressed. I noticed that my son likes to go to school here. On the other hand, in Russia he was always looking forward to the next school break.

Although Albert Shanker presented good arguments in favor of establishing a national curriculum in the U.S., there are some disadvantages as well. The ability to make a personal choice is one important part of freedom. We should consider all the facts before acting.

Yulia Amicci

**Points to note:**

1. The first sentence contains the author's name, title of the article and the main idea.

2. There is a summary of the main points of the reading in the writer's own words.

3. There is a transition sentence from the summary to the thesis statement.

4. The thesis statement clearly gives the topic and the main ideas of the body.

5. The introductory paragraph (summary + thesis) is not more than one quarter of the entire essay.

6. Each of the body paragraphs contains a topic sentence.

7. The body paragraphs are developed with detailed explanations and specific examples.

8. The conclusion expresses a clear opinion and restates the main idea of the essay. It synthesizes the main ideas of the writer and the author of the article.

Exercise 14

Read the article "Chinese Medicine for American Schools", by Nicholas Kristof, on pages 125 – 126 of the *Handbook*. Choose one of the following questions and write a reading response essay. Fill out the outline on this page before you write.

---

1. **Chinese students don't appear to have much free time during their school years. Do you think this is a good thing or a bad thing?**

2. **Do you agree with Nicholas Kristof that the American education system is not challenging enough? Explain your answer using examples.**

3. **Is it important for the American educational system to focus more on math and science? How can we get more students to be interested in these subjects?**

---

Outline

Introductory paragraph
1.    Summary of article contents:


2.    Thesis statement:


Body paragraphs
Major points (List by number; sketch out some details and examples):  ,









Concluding paragraph

# THE RESEARCH PAPER

## Purpose of the Research Paper

A research paper includes ideas from other people's speech or writing. Since you did not originate these ideas, you must acknowledge them with proper documentation. Even a short research paper must include a list of works cited. Like your other papers, it should be typed double-spaced. Your instructor should specify the minimum number of pages and sources you need to use in your paper.

You may begin your research by going to the **library** or the **internet**. There, you will search for the information that you need. Find sources that fit your topic and write **notes** in the margins of any material you might use. Use your sources (periodical articles, interviews, the internet, etc.) as specific support for the arguments that you make in your research paper.

Source information can be presented in three ways: by **quoting** the exact words from a source; by **paraphrasing** a statement in your own words; or by **summarizing** another author's ideas, whether they be from a single paragraph or an entire article.

Whichever method you use to present another author's ideas, you must **document** the source so that the reader knows where you found the information.

The purpose of the research paper in an advanced writing class is to familiarize students with the basic conventions of college writing. You may be asked to write research papers in many different subject areas. In addition, students must become familiar with the conventions surrounding other people's original ideas. Never use another writer's original idea without also citing his or her name and the source publication. If you use other people's ideas without citing your sources, you are **plagiarizing**.

Remember also that in any paper you write, **your** ideas are the most important. Good research is the basis and support for your own original ideas. A good research paper is not simply a collection of other people's ideas, in the form of quotes and paraphrases, that are brought together in one paper. You need to devote most of your research paper to the development of your own ideas, which must be based on your thesis statement.

## Plagiarism

Plagiarism is the act of using another writer's words or ideas without documenting the source of the information. *Webster's New Collegiate Dictionary* defines the verb 'plagiarize' as follows:

> " TO STEAL AND PASS OFF (THE IDEAS AND WORDS OF ANOTHER) AS ONE'S OWN."

Plagiarizing, in other words, is seen as an act of **theft**. A plagiarizer **robs** another author of his or her ideas when he or she does not give that author credit.

**Colleges and universities treat cases of plagiarism very seriously. A student who has been caught plagiarizing may fail the course, or even be expelled from the institution.**

The key to avoiding plagiarism is good documentation of sources. Every time you use another author's ideas or words, use parenthetical documentation citing the author's name and the number of the page from which you got the information. In addition to showing your honesty, this documentation helps the reader to:

1)   find the sources of a writer's argument;

2)   do further reading on the subject by going back to the documented sources;

3)   understand the extent of the writer's research and the integrity of his or her approach.

## Research tools

The following are the most important research tools you will be using to get information for your research paper assignment.

---

1. **Your college or local library:**

   From the library's home page, you should be able to access many different sources of information:

   **The online card catalog** will allow you to look up book and periodical titles that the library has on its shelves.

   **An online periodical index,** such as EBSCOhost, will allow you to search for articles in current periodicals using key words.

   **A newspaper index,** such as one for *The New York Times*, will let you find articles in a particular newspaper. Look also for local newspaper indexes if you are researching a topic about your region.

   Your library's web site may also give access to many other online sources, such as **encyclopedias, government pages, directories, academic journals,** etc.

2. **The internet**

   Use a search engine, such as **Google** <http://www.google.com/>, to look for sources on the internet. Make sure that you carefully evaluate these sources before using them. Be especially cautious when using information from **blogs** or open-source web publications like **Wikipedia**.

3. **Personal interviews**

   You can use a face-to-face **meeting**, a **telephone**, a **survey**, or **e-mail** to interview people about your topic.

4. **Other kinds of sources:**

   These may include **TV programs** and **documentaries, brochures** and **pamphlets,** as well as class **textbooks**.

---

## Evaluating Sources

Always check your sources carefully. Remember that some writers are writing expressly to deceive. The internet is full of sites that seem to give important information, but they may have little value because:

a)   the information is biased and unbalanced;
b)   the information is intended to deceive;
c)   the information is false;
d)   the information is not serious (it's a 'joke' site);
e)   the sites are 'open source' or wikis that may not be fully researched;
f)   the sites do not give sources.

Thus, when using a source, try to ask the following questions:

| | |
|---|---|
| 1. | **Is the writer (person or organization) credible?** |
| 2. | **Is the article or website objective?** |
| 3. | **Is the information current?** |
| 4. | **Are the writer's sources specifically cited? Are they credible sources?** |
| 5. | **Can you verify the sources or other information?** |

You should be able to answer YES to at least three of these questions if your source is a good one.

In addition, you need to pay attention to the following:

| | |
|---|---|
| 1. | **Understand the audience and any political or ideological bias the source may have.** |
| 2. | **Understand the purpose (inform, educate, sell, persuade).** |
| 3. | **Understand the aspects of the topic which the source covers as well as what it does not cover.** |
| 4. | **Understand the period of time covered by the source.** |
| 5. | **On a website, check the links, which may lead to more valuable information.** |

## Note-taking

Once you have selected a suitable topic, you need to collect information from outside sources to supply the facts and examples which will support your argument. Use your library, the internet, or other sources to find material related to your topic.

When you have found a magazine article, encyclopedia entry, web page, or some other source related to your topic, make your own printed copy. Then, you should read through it carefully, **highlight important phrases** and **write notes in the margins**. It is very important to do this for several reasons: first, writing notes in your own words makes it easier for you to paraphrase; second, writing notes will highlight the information which is directly related to your paper; third, writing notes will help you to become familiar with your source material. Finally, don't just repeat important information in the margin, but write your <u>opinion</u> about this information.

You should establish a system for writing notes. Develop your own set of abbreviations and symbols so that you can write notes at speed. Write down only the most important words: nouns, verbs, statistics, names of people, places, dates. Function words like prepositions and articles are usually not noted down.

One system of writing notes uses each side of the paper for a different purpose:
1. **On the left side, repeat or summarize important information in note form.**
2. **On the right side, give your response or opinion.**

<u>Exercise 15</u>

Write quick notes for the following sentences from "Are American Schools Too Easy?" (pp. 104 - 105).

Example: "we find that they are far ahead of their U.S. counterparts because they are assigned more work and more challenging work"
*Other ss ahead of U.S. ss -> ass. more work, more chall.*

1. "Our 50 state governments have developed curriculum materials, but they are very broadly defined."


2. " . . . they teach a watered-down curriculum and shortchange youngsters who could learn if they were given a chance."


3. "Learning to write well or be competent in math is a lot like preparing for the Olympics."


4. "In the U.S., a teacher who pushes students to work hard is viewed as unreasonable or even mean."

Look at the note-taking examples in the excerpt below from the article "Are American Schools Too Easy?" (pp. 104 - 105).

*Example:*
*Russian ss*

      Recently I saw a TV interview with some Russian youngsters who now live in the U.S. After some standard questions, the interviewer asked them to compare their school experiences here with their experiences in Russia. Every one of these seventh and eighth graders

*U.S. schools*
*easy*

had the same response: They'd already learned the material they were getting in our seventh- and eighth-grade classes when they were in third or fourth grade in Russia. They said that school in the U.S. was very easy.

*Yes! I agree*

      There was nothing unusual about this exchange. Indeed, most people who have met foreign students from France or Germany or

*3 reasons:*

Japan have heard the same things. And if we question students like these a little further, we find that they are far ahead of their U.S.

*U.S. schools*
*are not so*
*challenging*

*1,*
*2, 3*

counterparts because they are assigned more work and more challenging work, and they work harder to get it all done. But why do they work harder? They have the same distractions as American

*Why?*

kids. They have TV sets and pop culture.

*Maybe more*
*discipline*

Note the following:

1.     The highlighting and notes in the left margin complement each other.

2.     The notes on the right side give opinions.

<u>Exercise 16</u>

Read the article "Are American Schools Too Easy?" on pages 104 - 105. Continue to highlight and write notes in both margins as in the example above.

# Are American Schools Too Easy?

**By Albert Shanker**

Recently I saw a TV interview with some Russian youngsters who now live in the U.S. After some standard questions, the interviewer asked them to compare their school experiences here with their experiences in Russia. Every one of these seventh and eighth graders had the same response: They'd already learned the material they were getting in our seventh- and eighth-grade classes when they were in third or fourth grade in Russia. They said that school in the U.S. was very easy.

There was nothing unusual about this exchange. Indeed, most people who have met foreign students from France or Germany or Japan have heard the same things. And if we question students like these a little further, we find that they are far ahead of their U.S. counterparts because they are assigned more work and more challenging work, and they work harder to get it all done. But why do they work harder? They have the same distractions as American kids. They have TV sets and pop culture.

One of the main reasons is that these other countries have national curriculums. They have decided what students need to know and be able to do by the time they graduate from secondary school. And they've worked back from these goals to figure out what children should learn by the time they are ages 14 and 9.

That's not true in the U.S. Our 50 state governments have developed curriculum materials, but they are very broadly defined. So each school or teacher can select from this broad array and develop what amounts to an individual curriculum.

This makes for plenty of variety but very little continuity. As a result, students who move from one school - or even one class - to another often find they are out of sync because they have not studied the math or history on which the coming year's work will be based. In countries where there is a national curriculum, fewer students are lost - and fewer teachers are lost because they know what the students who walk into their classroom have already studied.

A national curriculum gives everyone involved - students, parents and teachers - a different perspective on schoolwork. In the U.S., when a teacher piles on the work, students are likely to object. They say it's too hard and too much, and they complain that other teachers or other schools don't expect that kind of work. Often parents support these objections. So there is a process of negotiation about schoolwork in which students, and frequently parents, play a big role.

Sometimes teachers don't ask enough of students. They feel sorry for some youngsters because of their socioeconomic or racial or ethnic background and decide they won't be able to do real work. So they teach a watered-down curriculum and  shortchange youngsters who could learn if they were given a chance.

In our system, how much work students do in a given class is up for grabs. Sometimes it's determined by the willingness or resistance of students and parents. Sometimes it's based on the teacher's expectations. In any case, the level and amount of work common in countries with national curriculums is practically never reached here. The choices our system allows inevitably lead to softer standards and less work just as the mandates in other countries lead to more work and much higher levels of achievement. If a student or a parent in one of these countries does complain, the teacher says, "All the other third-grade youngsters are doing this work, and you can, too." And the teacher probably reminds the parents and child that falling behind now can lead to serious consequences later - like not passing an important exam.

Learning to write well or be competent in math is a lot like preparing for the Olympics. Youngsters have to work hard and do more than they think they can. This can be unpleasant and even border on the painful, but it takes this kind of stretching to achieve high levels in any field. In the U.S., a teacher who pushes students to work hard is viewed as unreasonable or even mean. But where there are external standards, a teacher is more like a coach - someone who is helping prepare kids for the Olympics - than like someone who has odd, personal ideas about education.

With a national curriculum, everybody knows what is required. If there also are clear and visible stakes - getting into university or an apprenticeship program - the pressure is on to make sure youngsters meet the standards. Without national standards and a national curriculum, there are no such pressures. That's why students in other countries work hard and do so well - and why students in our "easy" and undemanding schools do not. Knowing that should lead us to act.

# Quotes

Quoting a source lends authority to your argument. It also shows that you have consulted other sources. Quotes appear between **quotation marks** ( " . . . . . " ), and are usually **introduced by a statement** which may include the author and perhaps his or her title or position. You only need to do this the **first time** you use this source. A direct quotation may be introduced **objectively**, or reflect your **agreement or disagreement** with the author's opinion. Quotations are followed by a **parenthetical reference** which gives the **last name** of the author, if it is not already given in the introduction to the quote, and the **page number** of the quotation if the source is a hard copy of a periodical or book. Page numbers are not used for **web-based** sources. If **no author** is mentioned, you need to use the title, or the first part of the title, of the article or web page. See pages 127 - 129 for documentation of sources in your essay.

Here are some examples of quotations:

### 1. Objective:

According to Albert Shanker, former President of the American Federation of Teachers, "Learning to write well or be competent in math is a lot like preparing for the Olympics" (5). **OR**
"Learning to write well or be competent in math is a lot like preparing for the Olympics," according to Albert Shanker, former President of the American Federation of Teachers (5). **OR**
One expert even makes the following comparison: "Learning to write well or be competent in math is a lot like preparing for the Olympics" (Shanker 5).

### 2. Agreeing with the author:

Albert Shanker, former President of the American Federation of Teachers, makes an important point when he writes, "Learning to write well or be competent in math is a lot like preparing for the Olympics" (5).

### 3. Disagreeing with the author:

Albert Shanker, former President of the American Federation of Teachers, makes a misleading comparison when he writes, "Learning to write well or be competent in math is a lot like preparing for the Olympics" (5). **OR**
A former President of the American Federation of Teachers oversimplifies when he states, "Learning to write well or be competent in math is a lot like preparing for the Olympics" (Shanker 5).

Some verbs to use with quotes

| | | | |
|---|---|---|---|
| say | write | mention | argue |
| state | contend | assert | advocate |
| claim | believe | think | feel |

Punctuation in quotations

## 1. Comma vs. Colon

Short quotations should be preceded by a **comma** ( , ) or **colon** ( : ). A colon is used if the words preceding the quote form a complete sentence, for example:

> According to a former President of the American Federation of Teachers, "Learning to write well or be competent in math is a lot like preparing for the Olympics" (Shanker 5).

> Albert Shanker is an unabashed proponent of a national curriculum: "Learning to write well or be competent in math is a lot like preparing for the Olympics" (5).

## 2. Capitalization

The first word of a quotation is capitalized if the quote is a complete sentence.

## 3. Ellipsis

If you decide to leave some words out of an author's original statement, use ellipsis ( . . . ) to show that words have been left out, for example:

> According to a former President of the American Federation of Teachers, "Learning to write well . . . is a lot like preparing for the Olympics" (Shanker 5).

## 4. Brackets

Use brackets ( [   ] ) when you are inserting or substituting words in the quotation, for example:

> According to a former President of the American Federation of Teachers, "In [the American] system, how much work students do in a given class is up for grabs" (Shanker 5).

## 5. Punctuating Documentation

Parenthetical documentation follows the quotation and comes before the period (if the quotation ends a sentence). See page 127 - 129 for more details about documentation. Here is another example of a quote using ellipsis and brackets:

Original text:
"During the following stage children acquire the language to describe and define different groups. It is at this point that deep feelings and strong attitudes - both positive and negative - are often conveyed by parents and other significant adults."
Quote:
One expert on language acquisition asserts, "During the [second] stage children acquire the language to describe and define different groups. It is at this point that deep feelings and strong attitudes . . . are often conveyed by parents and other significant adults" (Katz 185).

## Questions about quoting

### 1. What is the purpose of quoting?

Quotes give your paper some authority. They show you have done some serious reading or research. They can be used as supporting information for your ideas.

### 2. When should I quote?

Quote when the author's own words seem particularly important, when an expert gives an interesting or controversial opinion, and when your own words (a paraphrase) cannot match the original meaning of the phrase. <u>Never use a writer's exact words without including them in quotation marks and documenting the source.</u>

### 3. How often should I quote?

The research paper is supposed to be based your own ideas. Use quotes to support your own explanations. In a short research paper, one or two quotes per body paragraph may be appropriate.

### 4. What does a quote look like?

The punctuation for quotes and some examples of quotes are discussed on pp. 103 – 104. <u>Never write a quote as a complete sentence</u> that is unconnected to a relevant introductory phrase.

### 5. How long should a quote be?

Quote part of a sentence, a single sentence, or perhaps a couple of short sentences at the most. You are just writing a short research paper and long quotes should not take up most of your paragraphs.

### 6. How do I include a quote in a paragraph?

Quotes need to fit into your paragraphs and support ideas that are already written. Use transition words and specific introductory phrases to lead into each quote (see p. 106).

See the next page for examples of good and bad paragraphs using quotes.

**Quoting: example of a bad paragraph**

Finally, what detractors have against the ratings system is that it tempts parents to let go of their responsibilities when it comes to television. "The networks, not the parents, decide what's best for every age group". (Gruenwald 424). Each parent has a different approach to violence, sex, or bad language, and for the networks to censor those is not the best solution. "There has to be some kind of renaissance of individual responsibility that's accepted by parents, by the church, and by the schools, so that you build inside a youngster what we call a moral shield - it's fortified by the Ten Commandments of God - so that that child understands what is right and what is clearly wrong." They should teach them to understand what they are watching instead of hiding it from them. Children are smart and always find a way to do what parents forbid. An explanation would be more efficient when it comes to violence, sex, and bad language. The ratings system doesn't work. "It identifies the violence, but it does not remove it. It puts the onus on the parents" (Mortimer Zuckerman 64).

Points to note

1. At least half the paragraph is in quotations – too much!
2. None of the quotes is introduced . They are written as separate sentences.
3. The punctuation for the documentation of the first quote is incorrect.
4. The second quote is not documented at all.
5. The second quote is too long.
6. The third quote is documented, but only the author's last name should be used.

**Quoting: example of a good paragraph**

Finally, what detractors have against the ratings system is that it tempts parents to let go of their responsibilities when it comes to television. Ken Conrad, senior Democrat from North Dakota, says: " . . . the networks, not the parents, decide what's best for every age group" (qtd. in Gruenwald 424). Each parent has a different approach to violence, sex, or bad language, and for the networks to censor those is not the best solution. Children will be in contact with those 'undesirable' scenes while at friends' houses or when they are alone. Parents should explain to children that what they see on movies, shows, or cartoons is not real, that it is pure fiction invented to entertain people. They should teach them to understand what they are watching instead of hiding it from them. Children are smart and always find a way to do what parents forbid. An explanation would be more efficient when it comes to violence, sex, and bad language. The children will be exposed to those problems sometime in their lives and, by knowing them and understanding them through the television and their parents, they will be armed to deal with them.

Points to note

1. There is only one quote in the paragraph and it is short.
2. The quote is punctuated and documented correctly.
3. There is an appropriate introduction for the quote.
4. The rest of the paragraph is the writer's own analysis and ideas.

Exercise 17

The following quotes need to be written into a complete sentence with an introductory phrase and correct parenthetical documentation if needed.

Pay attention to sources which are quoted in articles. Both the author of the article and the person who made the statement need to be mentioned. Also, sources with no author need to documented by their titles. See the standards for documentation of different sources on pp. 127 - 129.

1. "In theory, hearts, livers and kidneys from pigs should be suitable for transplantation into people because they are about the same size as those in humans." From "Of Mice and Men," article in *Maclean's* by Mark Nichols (found on EBSCOhost – no page number).

2. "Even at rush hour, most trips are not commute trips." From "Building More Roads Will Reduce Traffic Congestion," article in *Connections* by Ross Williams of Citizens for Sensible Transportation, page 11.

3. "Each year, thousands of people are injured by exposure or accident involving hazardous household products." From *Household Hazardous Waste*, web page constructed by Office of Waste Management, University of Missouri Outreach and Extension – no author.

4. "As adults these young people were frightened of failure, frightened of commitment." Judith Wallerstein, author of *The Unexpected Legacy of Divorce* quoted in the *Newsweek* article "Does Divorce Hurt Kids?" by Richard Corliss, page 40.

5. "DNA fingerprinting is used to diagnose inherited disorder in both prenatal and newborn babies in hospitals around the world." From *DNA Fingerprinting in Human Health and Society*, web page written by Dr. David F. Betsch, Biotechnology Training Programs, Inc.

# Paraphrases

Paraphrasing is the restatement of a phrase, sentence, or several sentences, in your own words.

It is convenient to paraphrase when you want to reword an author's words to fit your own style of writing. It also allows you to vary the method of presenting source material, so that you don't have too many quotes in your paper. Most summaries are, in effect, a series of paraphrases.

When paraphrasing you should always keep the full meaning and tone of the passage. Don't add any new information, and don't leave essential information out. Always remember to give the author's name after the paraphrase if you don't mention it earlier in the sentence. A paraphrase from a periodical also requires a page number unless it is an online periodical.

Paraphrasing is an excellent test of vocabulary skills and reading comprehension. Paraphrase when you are answering questions for reading comprehension, as well as when you are using source information for your papers.

Use the following methods to paraphrase:

### 1. Synonyms

You can substitute words for phrases, or phrases for words, or one word for another. **Always** make sure that you change the **form** of the sentence substantially.

Example:

Original:    "There are jobs out there that pay substantial amounts of money to people who don't have college degrees."
Paraphrase:  There are well-paid positions for those who haven't graduated from college (Pratt and Begnones 17).

### 2. Changing the parts of speech

You can change nouns to verbs, or adjectives to adverbs, etc.

Example:

Original:    "The collapse of communism and the end of the Cold War will mean a radical revision of the international order."
Paraphrase:  Since communism has collapsed and the Cold War has ended, the world order will be radically revised (*New World Order*).

## 3. Changing the word order in a sentence

Word order can be altered by changing from active to passive, changing the positions of phrases, etc.

Example:

Original: "For the last generation or two, psychiatrists have vigorously explored the sexual lives of children, the different kinds of family lives of children, the emotional disturbances of family life."

Paraphrase: The sexual lives of children, the different kinds of family lives they have, and their emotional problems have been intensely investigated by psychiatrists during the past few decades (Kritz 79).

## 4. Combining sentences

This can be done especially when the sentences are short.

Example:

Original: "We need to take care of the homeless and the poor, and attack drugs and crime. We must clean up our environment, rebuild our highways, railroads and merchant fleet."

Paraphrase: Americans must address the problems of homelessness, poverty, drugs, crime, the environment, and also reconstruct the highway, rail, and shipping systems ("The New Millenium").

## 5. Making long sentences short

Divide long sentences into shorter ones.

Example:

Original: "What has helped push tuition costs down, they say, has been the the increasing competitiveness among schools, a more cost-conscious national attitude and the widespread frustration with the standard practice of discounting prices through scholarships and other forms of aid, while keeping tuition high."

Paraphrase: Three reasons are given for the reduction in college tuition. First, there is more and more competition between colleges. Second, people are more aware of high costs. Third, people are frustrated with the colleges charging high tuition rates while they commonly offer scholarships and other kinds of financial aid (Applebome).

**Examples of good and bad paraphrases**

**Original:**

"However our health system evolves – with more government control or more market influence – Americans need to come to a more realistic understanding of its limits."

from: "Let's Not Hide Health Costs" by Robert J. Samuelson *Newsweek*, 5 February 2007: 52.

**Direct plagiarism:**

However our health system evolves – with more government control or more market influence – Americans need to come to a more realistic understanding of its limits.

*This is straight copying. No sources are given. The writer is plagiarizing.*

**Bad paraphrase/ plagiarism:**

However our health system develops – with more government control or more market influence – people need to come to a more realistic understanding of its limitations.

*Not enough changes - therefore, quotes should be used; no citation. This would also be considered plagiarism even though a few words have been changed.*

**A little better, but not good enough:**

It doesn't matter how our health system develops, whether under more government influence or through market influence, Americans need to come to a more realistic understanding of its limitations. (Samuelson 52)

*More changes, but maybe not enough; citation has incorrect punctuation (period after parentheses).*

**Good paraphrase:**

People in the U.S. must be more realistic about the limitations of the American system of health care no matter whether the changes come from government regulations or the economic pressures of supply and demand (Samuelson 52).

*Good, extensive changes without changing the essential meaning; accurate citation with proper punctuation.*

Exercise 18

Circle the best paraphrase for each of the following quotes.

1. Original quote: "According to an AAUW study, "When boys and girls are in the same classroom, . . . boys speak out more and teachers call on them more often to answer questions" (Dornin).

Which is the best paraphrase of the ideas of the original quote?

A. When boys and girls are in the same classroom, males speak up more and instructors call on them more often to answer questions (Dornin).

B. Because males are more aggressive and louder, teachers pay more attention to them than they pay attention to girls (Dornin).

C. Girls don't talk much in classes with boys (Dornin).

D. In coed classes, boys talk more than girls, according to a report, and instructors ask boys questions more frequently (Dornin).

E. I think it is too bad that girls don't talk much around boys when they are together in class, but that is the way people are (Dornin).


2. Original quote: "A new analysis has found that in the majority of trials conducted by drug companies in recent decades, sugar pills have done as well – or better than – antidepressants" (Mercola).

Which is the best paraphrase of the ideas of the original quote?

A. Sugar pills are better than antidepressants, according to some drug companies (Mercola).

B. A new study has found that most trials conducted by drug companies in recent decades show that sugar pills have performed as well as antidepressants (Mercola).

C. Many studies indicate that antidepressants are as good as sugar pills (Mercola).

D. Sugar pills have an equal or better effect than antidepressants, according to a review of studies done by pharmaceutical corporations (Mercola).

E. Sugar pills are the best way to cure depression, according to many trials conducted by drug companies (Mercola).

## Questions about paraphrasing

### 1. What is the purpose of paraphrasing?
Like quotes, paraphrases give your paper some authority and attest to the quality of your research. They can be used as supporting information for your ideas.

### 2. When should I paraphrase and when should I quote?
If you already have one quote in a paragraph, you may wish to paraphrase your next source. You don't want to quote too much. <u>Never paraphrase without documenting the source</u>.

### 3. How often should I paraphrase?
Most of the paragraph should be your own ideas. Paraphrase when you want to express someone's precise opinion, but use only one or two paraphrases and quotes per paragraph.

### 4. What kind of paraphrase should I use?
It's up to you. Usually you will use a combination of the methods outlined on pp. 111 – 112.

### 5. What does a paraphrase look like?
Paraphrases do not have special punctuation. They should be introduced with the appropriate information about their origin. They must be documented correctly, for example:

Original text:
> "Learning to write well or be competent in math is a lot like preparing for the Olympics."

Paraphrase:
> Albert Shanker, former President of the American Federation of Teachers, asserts that becoming good at writing or math is like getting ready for the Olympic Games (5).

### 6. How do I include a paraphrase in a paragraph?

Like quotes, paraphrases need to fit into your paragraphs and support ideas that are already written. Use transition words and specific introductory phrases.

Here is an example of a paragraph from a student research paper. It includes two paraphrases from different sources:

Marijuana's ability to stimulate appetite, known to mankind for centuries, is particularly significant now in the treatment of AIDS. A large number of patients with AIDS smoke marijuana to combat the human immunodeficiency virus infection and associated wasting syndrome. Smoking appears to be more effective in enhancing appetite than taking THC in the capsule form. Even though insurance will pay for synthetic version of THC, some patients spend their money and risk breaking the law for the more effective marijuana (Conant). The best alternative to smoked marijuana for combating AIDS-related wasting is human growth hormone, which has been found to restore muscle and improve chances of survival. However, the cost of this hormone for a year's supply is $ 36,000, whereas marijuana treatment for the same period costs $500 ("Marijuana as a Medicine").

**Margarita Vainiene**

Exercise 19

Follow the patterns to help you paraphrase the **c** sentence in each set.

1.  a. "A recent study showed that listening to jazz causes baldness" (Van Zyl).
    b. According to a recent study, you may go bald if you listen to jazz (Van Zyl).

    c. "Smith's experiment showed that jogging caused craziness" (Rogers).

    d. _____

    _____

2.  a. "When they reach adulthood, young smokers may become chain smokers" (Han 23).
    b. In adulthood, young smokers sometimes become chain smokers (Han 23).

    c. "When they become old, joggers may have foot problems" (Mastriola 117).

    d. _____

    _____

3.  a. "Although there is a big unemployment problem, nothing has been done by the government" (*Workers Unite*)
    b. In spite of the great unemployment problem, the government has done nothing (*Workers Unite*).

    c. "Although there is a crisis, nothing has been done by the administration" (*Congress Debates War*)

    d. _____

    _____

4.  a. "For the most part, citizens believe that teachers are hard workers" ("System in Crisis Mode").
    b. Citizens generally believe that teachers work hard ("System in Crisis Mode").

    c. "For the most part, voters believe that politicians are good speakers" ("Election Polarizes District").

    d. _____

    _____

5.  a. "This kind of problem might be found anywhere" (Campbell and Suarez).
    b. We can find problems like this anywhere (Campbell and Suarez).

c. "That kind of citizen can be depended on" (Pogue and DuLay).

d. _____

_____

6.   a. "An unemployed person has difficulty keeping up hope" (*On the Line*).
     b. It is hard for a person who is unemployed to remain hopeful (*On the Line*).

     c. "A retired person usually has no difficulty continuing an active life" (*Good Times*).

     d. _____

     _____

7.   a. "He recovered from his illness. Then, he took a two-week break from work"
        ("Stress a Major Factor in Productivity Decline").
     b. He didn't work for two weeks after recovering from his illness ("Stress a Major
        Factor in Productivity Decline").

     c. "They returned from vacation. After that, they spent a few days getting
        organized" ("Cross-country Move Changes Perspective").

     d. _____

     _____

8.   a. "In the opinion of many experts, there are several problems which can result
        from watching too much television, including the ideas that TV shows can
        contribute to the forming of sex stereotypes, watching violence on TV may
        lead to similarly violent behavior, TV watching takes times away from play
        and reading, and frightening shows may cause nightmares" (Engstrom and Cho).
     b. Experts note that TV watching may cause several problems. First, sex
        stereotypes may be formed from certain ideas on TV shows. Second, violent
        behavior may result from watching violence on TV Third, play and reading
        time may be diminished by watching TV Fourth, nightmares may be caused
        by watching frightening shows (Engstrom and Cho).
     c. "Before calling the police, you can go through several steps in dealing with a
        problem neighbor; for example you can try to talk to the neighbor and listen to
        his or her side of the story, or you can contact your Neighborhood Mediation
        Office, or you can get your Neighborhood Association to write the neighbor a letter"
        (Ramirez and Valenzuela).

     d. _____

     _____

Exercise 20

The following methods are used to paraphrase another writer's idea(s) in your own words:

- Using synonyms
- Changing the parts of speech
- Changing the word order
- Combining sentences
- Making long sentences short

Using a combination of methods (not just one method) paraphrase the following sentences. Be careful not to leave out information or alter the meanings of the sentences.

1. "Many environmentalists say that solar and wind power have the greatest potential for growth and for displacing fuels that cause pollution and are suspected of causing changes in the world's climate" (Langsdale).

_____

_____

_____

_____

_____

2. Though credit cards are still used for the majority of non-eBay purchases, alternatives such as Bill Me Later, Google Checkout and PayPal are expected to gain market share (*Online Malls*).

_____

_____

_____

_____

_____

3. Most of the growth among women and minorities hired as college presidents has been at community colleges, not four-year institutions, according to a survey by the American Council on Education (Phillips and Nowak).

_____

_____

_____

_____

_____

4. Generally, the best educational software programs for home use integrate fun with learning so smoothly that children will hardly realize that they are learning (Hearst 35).

_____

_____

_____

_____

_____

5. An analysis of the mouse genome that was published recently by an international consortium is important because only by comparing the human genome with those of other species can scientists extract the fullest understanding of how genes operate. Best of all, mouse genes can be easily manipulated in the laboratory, making it possible to conduct genetic experiments that would be ethically objectionable to perform on people ("Cloning Takes a New Turn").

_____

_____

_____

_____

_____

Exercise 21

These are the same quotes as in the exercise on page 110. Now try to paraphrase them using an appropriate introductory phrase and the correct documentation in parentheses. See the section on documenting sources on pages 127-129.

1. "In theory, hearts livers and kidneys from pigs should be suitable for transplantation into people because they are about the same size as those in humans." From "Of Mice and Men," article in *Maclean's* by Mark Nichols (found on EBSCOhost periodical index – no page number).

2. "Even at rush hour, most trips are not commute trips."
From "Building More Roads Will Reduce Traffic Congestion," article in *Connections* by Ross Williams of Citizens for Sensible Transportation, page 11.

3. "Each year, thousands of people are injured by exposure or accident involving hazardous household products."
From *Household Hazardous Waste*, web page constructed by Office of Waste Management, University of Missouri Outreach and Extension – no author.

4. "As adults these young people were frightened of failure, frightened of commitment."
Judith Wallerstein, author of *The Unexpected Legacy of Divorce* quoted in the *Newsweek* article "Does Divorce Hurt Kids?" by Richard Corliss, page 40.

5. "DNA fingerprinting is used to diagnose inherited disorder in both prenatal and newborn babies in hospitals around the world."
From *DNA Fingerprinting in Human Health and Society*, web page written by Dr. David F. Betsch, Biotechnology Training Programs, Inc.

# Short Summaries

In a paraphrase, a writer expresses another author's exact ideas using different words; however, in a summary the writer must decide which material to use and which to leave out. Most summaries make a passage shorter by keeping only the main ideas. You can summarize a paragraph or an entire article. A summary in a short research paper should not be more than three to five sentences in length.

The steps to be followed in summarizing a passage:

1.   Understand clearly the content and organization of the passage.

2.   Find the main idea. Sometimes, a paraphrase of the main idea is sufficient to convey the author's meaning.

3.   If more than a paraphrase of the topic sentence is needed, look at the organization of the passage and take notes based on an outline:

     I. Main idea (thesis)

     II. Important aspects of the main idea
         (Leave out details and examples)

     III. Author's conclusions

4.   Don't include examples unless they are necessary to an understanding of the author's idea.

5.   Write your summary using only the outline you have made. **Don't look at the original article,** or you may find yourself copying word for word.

6.   If you wish, begin your summary with a reference to the author, followed by the author's thesis. Use the present tense when introducing an author's statement, for example:

     Smith states that . . .
     Smith points out that . . .
     Robert Smith concludes that . . .
     According to Robert Smith, . . .

7.   Remember to document your source in parentheses after your summary, or mention the source in an introductory phrase.

## Example of a summary

The following are notes written from the article "Are American Schools Too Easy?" which appears on pages 104 - 105 of this handbook.

---

*Intro:*   *TV int. w/Russ. Ss in U.S.: school in U.S. v. easy*
    *Foreign Ss ahead of U.S. -*    *more work*
            *more chall. work*
            *work harder*

*WHY? (same pop. culture as U.S.)*
*ANSWER:*        **National curriculums**
    *In U.S.:*    *50 states, curr. broadly defined, ea. school/T selects*
        *=*    *lots of variety, little continuity*
            *Ss who move fr. 1 sch. -> another "out of sync"*
            *(not true in countries w/nat. curr.)*
    *Nat curr:*    *Ss, Ts, parents all involved*

    *U.S.:*    *T. gives more hw: Ss object; s/times parents too*
            *Ts don't ask enough: feel sorry for Ss w/ racial/ethnic*
                        *background*
            *Quantity of work not fixed*
            *Too many choices = lower standards*

    *Other countries:*
            *More work -> higher achieve.*
            *If Ss/parents complain -> "everyone else doing this"*

*Good writing/math skills = like prep. for Olympics*
            *Can be unpleas., but -> high achiev.*
*In U.S., T. who pushes s/times "unreasonable"*

*W/Nat. curr.:*        *T = coach*
            *Everyone knows require.*
            *Clear goals*

*W/O Nat curr.*        *no pressures, no hard work*

*Shanker: we should act*

Here is a possible short summary of the article:

> *Albert Shanker, writing in On Campus, asserts that schools in countries which have national curriculums have higher standards than schools in the U.S., which do not follow a national curriculum. In the U.S., students who move from one school to another may have a hard time adapting to the new curriculum. In addition, if U.S. teachers try to give more homework, students might complain and their parents may support them. Teachers may not challenge their students enough because they have sympathy for those from disadvantaged backgrounds. In the U.S., the quantity of work is not fixed. The U.S., therefore, offers many choices but also lower standards. In other countries, students do more work and display higher achievement because there are clear goals (Shanker 4).*

Here is a summary of one part of the article (effects of having no national curriculum in the U.S.):

> *Because there is no national curriculum in the U.S., students who move from one school to another may have a hard time adapting to the new curriculum. In addition, if U.S. teachers try to give more homework, students might complain and their parents may support them. Teachers may not challenge their students enough because they have sympathy for those from disadvantaged backgrounds. In the U.S., the quantity of work is not fixed. (Shanker 4).*

Exercise 22

Read the article "Chinese Medicine for American Schools"* on the following pages. Try to make an outline of the main ideas of the article. Use the plan below to help you. Some of the ideas have already been provided.


I.    Main idea:



II.    Important aspects of the main idea

       A. Author's personal experience with daughter:

       _____

       _____

       B. Why Chinese education is more successful:
           1. _____
           2. _____
           3. _____
           4. _____
           5. _____
           6. _____

       C. Solutions for the U.S.:
           1. _____
           2. _____


Exercise 23

Now try to write a brief summary of the article from your notes. Remember that you can choose the points you wish to emphasize in your summary.


* Originally published in *The New York Times*, June 27th, 2006. Used with permission.

# Chinese Medicine for American Schools

## by Nicholas D. Kristof.
*The New York Times* (Late Edition (East Coast)): June 27th, 2006. A17.

Visitors to China are always astonished by the new highways and skyscrapers, and by the endless construction projects that make China's national bird the crane.

But the investments in China's modernization that are most impressive of all are in human capital. The blunt fact is that many young Chinese in cities like Shanghai or Beijing get a better elementary and high school education than Americans do. That's a reality that should embarrass us and stir us to seek lessons from China.

On this trip I brought with me a specialist on American third-grade education -- my third-grade daughter. Together we sat in on third-grade classes in urban Shanghai and in a rural village near the Great Wall. In math, science and foreign languages, the Chinese students were far ahead.

My daughter was mortified when I showed a group of Shanghai teachers some of the homework she had brought along. Their verdict: first-grade level at a Shanghai school.

Granted, China's education system has lots of problems. Universities are mostly awful, and in rural areas it's normally impossible to hold even a primitive conversation in English with an English teacher. But kids in the good schools in Chinese cities are leaving our children in the dust.

Last month, the Asia Society published an excellent report, "Math and Science Education in a Global Age: What the U.S. Can Learn from China." It notes that China educates 20 percent of the world's students with 2 percent of the world's education resources. And the report finds many potential lessons in China's rigorous math and science programs.

Yet, there isn't any magic to it. One reason Chinese students learn more math and science than Americans is that they work harder at it. They spend twice as many hours studying, in school and out, as Americans.

Chinese students, for example, must do several hours of homework each day during their summer vacation, which lasts just two months. In contrast, American students have to spend each September relearning what they forgot over the summer.

China's government has developed a solid national curriculum, so that nearly all high school students study advanced biology and calculus. In contrast, only 13 percent of American high school pupils study calculus, and fewer than 18 percent take advanced biology.

Yet if the Chinese government takes math and science seriously, children and parents do so even more. At Cao Guangbiao elementary school in Shanghai, I asked a third-grade girl, Li Shuyan, her daily schedule. She gets up at 6:30 a.m. and spends the rest of the day studying or practicing her two musical instruments.

So if she gets her work done and has time in the evening, does she watch TV or hang out with friends? "No," she said, "then I review my work and do extra exercises."

A classmate, Jiang Xiuyuan, said that during summer vacation, his father allows him to watch television each evening - for 10 minutes.

The Chinese students get even more driven in high school, as they prepare for the national college entrance exams. Yang Luyi, a ninth grader at the first-rate Shanghai High School, said that even on weekends he avoided going to movies. "Going to the cinema is time-consuming," he noted, "so when all the other students are working so diligently, how can you do something so irrelevant?"

And romance?

Li Yafeng, a ninth-grade girl at the same school, giggled at my question. "I never planned to have a boyfriend in high school," she said, "because it's a waste of time."

Now, I don't want such a pressured childhood for my children. But if Chinese go overboard in one direction, we Americans go overboard in the other. U.S. children average 900 hours a year in class and 1,023 hours in front of a television.

I don't think we could replicate the Chinese students' drive even if we wanted to. But there are lessons we can learn -like the need to shorten summer vacations and to put far more emphasis on math and science. A central challenge for this century will be how to regulate genetic tinkering with the human species; educated Chinese are probably better equipped to make those kinds of decisions than educated Americans.

During the Qing Dynasty that ended in 1912, China was slow to learn lessons from abroad and adjust its curriculum, and it paid the price in its inability to compete with Western powers. These days, the tables are turned, and now we need to learn from China.

# Documentation of Sources

Whenever you quote, paraphrase, or summarize from a source such as a newspaper or magazine article, web page, encyclopedia entry, interview, or book, you must **document your source** so that the reader knows where you found your information.

Documentation in the body of your paper can be done in one of two ways. One way is to put the author's last name in parentheses after a quote, paraphrase or short summary. Another way is to use the author's name (often the full name) in the introductory phrase of a sentence which contains a quote or a paraphrase. If your source is a regular periodical or book, you need to include the number of the page in parentheses at the end of the sentence. Sources from the Internet, including articles from a library's periodical index, usually have no page numbers. Sources which have no author mentioned must be cited using their title. Long titles of web pages and articles can be shortened to the first few words.

You do not need to supply the name of the magazine, date, or publisher. The reader can discover this information when he or she turns to the list of **works cited** at the end of your paper. On this page, sources are listed alphabetically so that it is easy to locate the source by the author's last name.

*Note* :     Some instructors may require different forms of documentation, such as footnotes, and different fields of study may use different conventions for documentation. Ask your instructor to explain which system he or she uses.

To review, do the following when quoting, paraphrasing or summarizing a source in the body of your paper:

> 1. **Put the author's <u>last name</u> in parentheses at the end of the sentence in which you quote or paraphrase.**
>
>    **OR**
>
>    **Mention the author's <u>full name</u> in the introductory phrase before the quote or paraphrase.**
>
> 2. **If your source is not off the Internet, include the page number of the original sentence(s) in parentheses at the end of your sentence.**
>
> 3. **If your source does not mention an author, put its title, or the first few words of the title, in parentheses after the quote or paraphrase.**

**Examples of documentation in the body of your paper:**

Here are some examples of citation methods for different kinds of sources. Citation methods will be similar for quotes and paraphrases. Note the **punctuation** for parenthetical references (period comes **after** the parentheses). Sources from the Internet do not have page numbers.

**1. Newspaper, magazine or book:**

Dan Koeppel, writing about China's bicycle culture, states: " . . . all the way into the 1990s, the Flying Pigeon was the most popular vehicle on earth" (62).   **OR**

Since the 1949 Revolution and " . . . all the way into the 1990s, the Flying Pigeon was the most popular vehicle on earth" (Koeppel 62).

**2. Online periodical or article in an online periodical index, such as EBSCOhost:**

Peter Pietromonaco, writing in *Poptronics*, describes the process thus: "Once you press that SEND button, your e-mail . . . basically takes the scenic route, dotted with overlooks and pit-stops – until it reaches its final destination."   **OR**

A simple e-mail message takes a winding and hazardous path: "Once you press that SEND button, your e-mail . . . basically takes the scenic route, dotted with overlooks and pit-stops – until it reaches its final destination" (Pietromonaco).

**3. Article or book with two or three authors:**

Indeed, Mark Mazzetti and David Cloud confirm, "Secret detention of terrorism suspects has been widely criticized by human rights organizations and foreign governments as a violation of international law that relied on interrogation methods verging on torture" (A9).   **OR**

Experts acknowledge, "Secret detention of terrorism suspects has been widely criticized by human rights organizations and foreign governments as a violation of international law that relied on interrogation methods verging on torture" (Mazzetti and Cloud A9).

**4. Article or book with more than three authors:**

Naughton et al. point out that "In addition to taking different technological paths, Toyota and GM have taken different approaches toward expansion in the U.S. market."

Observers of the industry recognize: "In addition to taking different technological paths, Toyota and GM have taken different approaches toward expansion in the U.S. market" (Naughton et al.).

et al. = et alii, from Latin meaning "and others"

## 5. Article with no author mentioned:

According to the Sentencing Commission, " It takes a hundred times the amount of powder cocaine to result in the same prison term as for crack" ("U.S. Commission").

> Full title of the article is: "U.S. Commission Advises Repeal of Crack Penalty"

## 6. Source quoted in another source:

George Seidel, a cloning expert at Colorado State University, says, "The more we understand about cloning, . . . the closer we are to replicating humans" (qtd. in Nichols).

> qtd. in = quoted in

## 7. Web page with author:

As Dr. David F. Betsch of Biotechnology Training Programs, states, " . . . a DNA fingerprint is the same for every cell, tissue, and organ of a person." **OR**

It is important to understand that," . . . a DNA fingerprint is the same for every cell, tissue, and organ of a person" (Betsch).

## 8. Web page with no author mentioned:

It must be emphasized that, " . . . both the total amount of sun received over the years, and overexposure resulting in sunburn can cause skin cancer" (*Introduction to Skin Cancer*).

## 9. Personal interview

A Windows dealer, Charles Huynh, interviewed on January 12th, 2008, said, "External hard drives allow for much greater storage capacity but may be more prone to breakdown than DVDs." **OR**

I interviewed a Windows dealer on January 12th, 2008, who said, " External hard drives allow for much greater storage capacity but may be more prone to breakdown than DVDs " (Huynh).

# Special Punctuation Notes

1.  Titles of books and websites, and names of periodicals should be in *italics*, for example:

    | | |
    |---|---|
    | *The Da Vinci Code* | (novel) |
    | *Encyclopedia Americana* | (encyclopedia) |
    | *Stumbling on Happiness* | (book) |
    | *National Geographic* | (monthly magazine) |
    | *U.S. News & World Report* | (weekly magazine) |
    | *Chicago Tribune* | (daily newspaper) |
    | *Returning Salmon by Restoring Rivers* | (website) |

2.  Names of articles should be put in quotations, for example:

    "Cooking Fish Southern Style"
    "Report Faults Use of Data on Air Travel"
    "Using Your Home as an Investment"
    "Riders Throttle Safety Legislation."

3.  Names of sacred writing are not underlined or put in quotation marks, for example:

    the Bible
    the Koran
    the Talmud
    the Upanishads

4.  Parenthetical documentation in the text always comes **before** the period, for example:

    "My child has watched cartoon shows such as *He-Man* and *The Master of the Universe* and *G.I. Joe* and his behavior is markedly more aggressive and violent after viewing these shows" (Glamour 89).

    "Many people would give anything to have a clone, mostly from fear of dying" (Walton).

    "Our research also suggests that difficulties in turning down one's emotions after a stressful event may be a major factor leading to adolescent mood disorders" (Dahl 18).

5.  Articles, web pages, etc. without an author indicated should be cited using the title of the article, or the first few words in the title, for example:

    "The family-friendly policies introduced by some companies with much fanfare - job sharing, flexible hours and the like - often don't hold up in practice" ("The Myth of Quality Time").

# The Works Cited Page

The works cited page is the last page of your research paper. It includes all the sources cited in your paper. These should be listed in alphabetical order, according to the author's last name or title of the source if there is no author. Sometimes an instructors may require a **bibliography,** which is a complete list of all the sources you have consulted, including those which are not cited in your paper.

This handbook follows the style of documentation recommended by the M.L.A. (Modern Language Association). A good web site for a comprehensive overview of documentation of sources is the "Humanities" section of Bedford St. Martin's *Research and Documentation Online* by Diana Hacker at: **http://www.dianahacker.com/resdoc/**

Also, an easy way to get complete citations for your sources is to use the free site offered by Easybibb at: **http://www.easybib.com/.** On Easybib, you can enter all the details of your source and then Easybib will produce a citation for your works cited page (Please note that this resource does not compose every kind of citation according to M.L.A. style).

Each type of source, such as a periodical, web site, or interview, requires its own special way of being listed. Some standards are:

1. **Alphabetize all your sources by author's last name OR by the title of the source if there is no author.**

2. **The works cited page is double-spaced like the rest of your paper.**

3. **The second, third, etc., lines of a citation are indented by five spaces or 1/2 inch.**

4. **Capitalize all words in a title except for articles and short prepositions.**

5. **Pay attention to the punctuation! Each type of source is cited differently.**

6. **Web sources, except for those from a subscription service such as EBSCOhost, require the complete URL (Universal Reference Locator). You should copy and paste the URL directly from your browser's address bar into your document.**

7. **If the URL is too long to fit on a line in your citation, make a space so that the remainder of the URL goes to the next line. URLs are shown in angle brackets < >.**

8. **All web sources require the date that you accessed the information.**

## Sources on the Internet

### 1. Entire web site (with author)

Harris, Bill. *How Noise-canceling Headphones Work.* 2007. How Stuff Works. 25 Feb.

2008 <http://electronics.howstuffworks.com/noise-canceling-headphone.htm>.

> Author's last name, first name. *Title of web site.* Date (if present). Name of organization
> that created the site. Date you accessed the site <complete URL>.

### 2. Entire web site (author unknown)

*Household Hazardous Waste.* 30 Nov. 2005. Office of Waste Management, U. of

Missouri Outreach and Extension. 5 Oct. 2007 <http://outreach.missouri.edu/

owm/hhw.htm>.

> *Title of web site.* Date (if present). Name of organization that created the site.
> Date you accessed the site <complete URL>.

### 3. Web site with a corporation or group as the author

American Academy of Pediatrics. *Car Safety Seats: A Guide for Families 2007.* 2007. 4 Apr.

2008 <http://www.aap.org/family/carseatguide.htm>.

> Name of company or group. *Title of web site.* Date (if present).
> Date you accessed the site <complete URL>.

### 4. Government web site

United States. Census Bureau. *Overview of Race and Hispanic Origin.* March 2001. 16 Dec.

2006 <http://www.census.gov/prod/2001pubs/c2kbr01-1.pdf>.

> Country. Government department. *Title of web site.* Date. Date you accessed the site <complete URL>.

### 5. Article or page from a web site (with author)

Ramsland, Kate. "Robert K. Ressler: Taking on the Monsters." *The Criminal Mind.* 2001.

Crime Library. 8 Oct. 2007 <http://www.crimelibrary.com/forensics/ressler/>.

> Author's last name, first name. "Title of web page." *Name of web site.* Date (if present).
> Name of organization that created the site. Date you accessed the site <complete URL>.

## 6. Article or page from a web site (author unknown)

"Spying on the Home Front." *Frontline*. 2007. PBS Online. 11 Jun. 2007

<http://www.pbs.org/wgbh/pages/frontline/homefront/?campaign=

pbshomefeatures_2_frontlinebrspyingonthehomefront_2007-05-16>.

> "Title of web page". *Title of web site*. Date. Name of organization.
> Date you accessed the site <complete URL>

## 7. Online newspaper

Goodman, Cindy Krischer. "New Grads Need Juggling Skills." *Miami Herald* 16 May

2007. 28 Jul. 2007 <http://www.miamiherald.com/103/story/108164.html>.

> Author's last name, first name. "Title of article." *Name of newspaper* date.
> Date you accessed the site <complete URL>.

## 8. Article from a library-subscribed periodical index

Lavelle, Marianne. "Taking Lumps at the Pump." *U.S. News and World Report* 30 Apr.

2007: 64 – 65. *MasterFile Premier*. EBSCOhost. Pandora Community College

Library, Pandora, AK. 24 Aug. 2007 <http://search.epnet.com>.

> Author's last name, first name. "Title of article." *Name of newspaper* date: page number(s).
> *Name of index or database*. Name of subscription service.  Name and place of library.
> Date you accessed the site <URL of subscription service>

## 9. Article from a library-subscribed periodical index (no author)

"Gore Warns Congressional Panels of 'Planetary Emergency' on Global Warming."

*New York Times* 22 Mar. 2007, late ed. (East Coast): A20. ProQuest. Stanwyck

University Library, Blantyre, WA. 6 Jan. 2008 <http://www.proquest.com>.

> "Title of article." *Name of newspaper* date, edition (if needed): page number(s). Name of
> subscription service. Name and place of library. Date you accessed the site
> <URL of subscription service>

## 10. Article from a library-subscribed database

Erdely, Sabrina Rubin. "Anorexia Can Strike Older Women." *Anorexia.* Ed. Karen F.

Balkin. At Issue Series. Greenhaven Press, 2005. *Opposing Viewpoints Resource*

*Center.* InfoTrac. University of Ambrosia Library, Carnalla, WI. 13 Oct. 2006

<http://infotrac.galegroup.com>.

Author's last name, first name . "Title of article." *Title of original source.* Editor or author of original
source. Name of series (if needed). Name of publisher, date of publication. *Name of online resource.*
Name of subscriptionservice. Name and place of library. Date you accessed the site
<URL of subscription service>

## 11. Online library-subscribed reference work, such as an encyclopedia

Jones, Ordie R. "Dry farming." *World Book Online Reference Center.* 2007. Langdon

College Library, Langdon, GA. 4 Apr. 2008.

Author's last name, first name. "Title of encyclopedia entry." *Name of reference work.* Date.
Name and place of library. Date you accessed the site.

## 12. A web source in a language other than English

Kurabayashi, Kazuo. "Koizumi souri no Yasukuni sanpai hyoumei to kakuryou no

sanpai wo sakeru ninshiki ni yoseru ichibun." *Zenkokusenyukairengou.* 25

Jun. 2001. 10 March 2006 <http://www.senyu-renjp/SENYU/01061.HTM>.

Author's last name, first name. "Transcribed title of web page or article." *Name of web sit*
*(transcribed).* Date (if present). Date you accessed the site <complete URL>.

## 13. Weblog (blog) posting

MasonM. "Open Season on Bicycles." Weblog post. 14 May 2007. JoeUser.com. 12 Sep.

2007 <http://masonm.joeuser.com/articles.asp?c=1&AID=152615>

Author's last name, first name (or author's blog name). "Title of blog posting." Weblog post.
Date of message. Name of forum. Date you accessed the site <complete URL>

## 14. E-mail message

Hwang, Tony. "Cougars Not Just in the Country ." E-mail to the author. 7 Apr. 2008.

Author's last name, first name. "Subject line of e-mail." Name of recipient. Date of message.

## Periodicals and Books

### 15. Article in a weekly magazine (with author)

Deveny, Kathleen. "Yummy vs. Slummy." *Newsweek* 13 Aug. 2007: 44 - 45.

> Author's last name, first name. "Title of article." *Name of magazine* date: page number(s).

### 16. Article in a monthly magazine (no author)

Hall, Stephen S. "Vesuvius: Asleep for Now." *National Geographic* Sep. 2007: 114 - 133.

> Author's last name, first name. "Title of article." *Name of magazine* date: page number(s).

### 17. Article in a daily newspaper

Hyland, Andy. "Feline Problem Not Isolated." *Kansas City Star* 3 Jan. 2007: B2.

> Author's last name, first name. "Title of article." *Name of newspaper* date: page number(s).

### 18. Article in a magazine or newspaper (no author)

"Don't Throw It Out!" *Scholastic Parent & Child* Apr. 2006: 8.

> "Title of article." *Name of periodical* date: page number(s).

### 19. Article in a magazine or newspaper with two or three authors

Talbott, Basil, and Fawn Johnson. "Gutierrez, Flake Introduce House Immigration Measure."

*Congress Daily* 22 Mar. 2007: 13.

> First author's last name, first name 'and' second author's first name last name.
> "Title of article." *Name of periodical* date: page number(s).

### 20. Editorial

"Mayor Should Keep Pushing For It." Editorial. *The Oregonian*, 16 May 2007: C6.

> "Title of article." Editorial. *Name of newspaper* date: page number.

### 21. Book

Jacot de Boinod, Adam. *The Meaning of Tingo*. New York: Penguin, 2006.

> Author's last name, first name. *Title of book*. Place of publication: Publisher, date.

## 22. Article or essay in an anthology

Ackerman, William V. "Casinos Have Proven Beneficial to Deadwood, South Dakota."

*Legalized Gambling.* Ed. Mary E. Williams. Contemporary Issues Companion

Series. San Diego: Greenhaven Press, 1999. 117 - 128.

Author's last name, first name. "Title of article." *Title of book.* Ed. Editor's first name last name.
Name of series (if needed). Place of publication: Publisher, date. Page numbers of article or essay.

## 23. Encyclopedia entry

Harrison, George R. "Spectroscopy." *The New Encyclopedia Britannica: Micropaedia.* 15th

ed., 2002.

Author's last name, first name. "Title of encyclopedia entry." *Name of encyclopedia..* Edition, date.

## 24. Dictionary entry

"Cyclone." *American Heritage Dictionary of the English Language.* 4th ed. 2001.

"Title of dictionary entry." *Name of dictionary..* Edition, date.

## Other Sources (TV, Interviews, etc.)

## 25. TV documentary program

*The Great Robot Race.* Nova. Public Broadcasting System. WGBH, Boston. 22 May 2007.

*Title of the documentary.* Name of the series. Name of the network.
Name and city of the station that produced the show. Date.

## 26. TV news story

Snow, Kate, rep. "What Are the Impacts of Immigration?." *World News Tonight.* ABC. ABC

News, New York. 17 May 2007.

Name of reporter, rep. "Title of story." *Title of program.* Name of the network.
Name and city of the station. Date.

## 27. Personal interview

Gomez, Claudia. Personal interview. 14 Jan. 2008.

Interviewee's last name, first name. Personal interview. Date.

**Example of a Works Cited Page**

Works Cited

Belyeu, Kathy and Christine Real de Azua. "Annual U.S. Wind Power Rankings Track Industry's Rapid Growth." *American Wind Energy Association.* 11 Apr. 2007. 21 Jun. 2007 <http://www.awea.org/newsroom/releases/Annual_US_Wind _Power _Rankings_041107.html>.

Flavin, Christopher. "The Use of Wind Power Should Be Increased." *Global Resources.* Ed. Charles P. Kozic. At Issue Series. Greenhaven Press, 2006. *Opposing Viewpoints Resource Center.* InfoTrac. Avila Community College Library, San Marta, CA. 26 Jun. 2007 <http://infotrac.galegroup.com>.

"Global Windpower Boom." *Modern Power Systems* Mar. 2007: 5. *MasterFile Premier.* EBSCOhost. Avila Community College Library, San Marta, CA.  24 Jun. 2007 <http://search.epnet.com>.

Smith, Rebecca. "The New Math of Alternative Energy." *Wall Street Journal* 12 Feb. 2007 (Eastern Ed.): R1 – R4.

United States. Department of Energy. *Wind and Hydropower Technologies Program.* Energy Efficiency and Renewable Energy. 30 Jan. 2007. 20 Jun. 2007 < http://www1.eere.energy.gov/windandhydro/>.

Wald, Matthew L. "Wind Farms May Not Lower Air Pollution, Study Suggests." *New York Times* 4 May 2007, late ed. (East Coast): A18. ProQuest. Avila Community College Library, San Marta, CA. 11 Jun. 2007 <http://www. proquest.com>.

Whipple, Dan. "The Birds and the Peetz Wind Farm." Weblog post. 17 May 2007. Colorado Confidential. 18 Jun. 2007 < http://www.coloradoconfidential.com/ showDiary.do?diaryId=2070>

**Name:** _____

<u>Final Essay Assignment: Research Paper</u>

## <u>Proposal</u>

### 1. Topic

I want to write about the following issue ( _____

_____ )

because _____

_____.

### 2. Stand

I am **FOR** **AGAINST** this issue. (circle one)

### 3. Thesis statement (shows topic + whether you are **FOR** or **AGAINST** + 'because' clause, e.g.

_____ should _____

because _____

### 4. List your main arguments:

1.

2.

3.

4.

5.

### 5. List the main arguments against your position:

1.

2.

3.

## Possible Problems with the Research Paper

## Review of Steps in Preparing the Research Paper

Writing a research paper is a lengthy process. Plan your research and writing Carefully.

| | | DATE DUE |
|---|---|---|
| I. | Select a topic. | _____ |
| II. | Narrow the topic. | _____ |
| III. | Find suitable sources: using the library, conducting interviews, etc. | _____ |
| IV. | Read and annotate sources; highlight possible quotes. | _____ |
| V. | Using the notes and your own ideas, write an outline. | _____ |
| VI. | Prepare the thesis statement. | _____ |
| VII. | Write a proposal (p. 137) | _____ |
| VIII. | Write the "rough" draft, with introduction, body paragraphs, and conclusion. Support body paragraphs with details, quotes, paraphrases. | _____ |
| IX. | Correct the "rough" draft and type a second draft. Check for cohesion. | _____ |
| X. | Type the final draft, including the works cited page. | _____ |

You may also be asked to **conference** with your instructor at some point in this process. Your instructor may ask you to bring a completed proposal and all your annotated sources to the conference.

Exercise 24

Review the *Advanced Writing Handbook for ESOL* to answer these questions.

1. Why do we have to document our sources when we write a research paper?

2. Where does the Works Cited page appear?

3. What is plagiarism?

4. What information should be on your title page?

5. What size of font should you use for the research paper?

6. How do you indicate the title of a web site or magazine in your paper?

7. How do you indicate the title of an article?

8. What is a URL?

9. How do you cite an article you found using a periodical index on the library's web site?

10. How do you cite an interview?

11. How do you document a magazine article in the text of your paper?

12. What is the recommended way to take notes?

Sun-Hwa Kim

Ms. Christina Sparks

ESOL 262: Level 8 Academic Writing

December 9th, 2006

Slots and Nature Don't Mix

The Columbia River Gorge is the beautiful scenic area in Oregon. Its cliffs, many waterfalls, beautiful scenery and wildlife have attracted many tourists. Also, people use the Columbia River Gorge for many recreational purposes: camping, hiking, wildlife viewing, and river travel. However, the Confederated Tribes of the Warm Springs Reservation of Oregon (the Tribe) have proposed building a mega-casino on an off-reservation site, Cascade Locks, in the Columbia River Gorge (the Gorge) because it is close to the Portland Metropolitan Area, the most lucrative and populated area in Oregon. The proposed casino complex, which will be the biggest and first off-reservation casino in Oregon, is a 600,000 square-foot facility that would include a casino, hotel, spa, restaurants and a conference center. Oregonians are debating whether building a casino in the Gorge is beneficial or harmful to them. The casino should not be built in the Gorge because it will cause many problems to Portland Metropolitan residents and destroy the beautiful scenery of the area.

First, building a casino in the Gorge violates Oregon's policy that limits each tribe to one casino on their reservation site (Wu). The tribe already has Kah-Nee-Ta Resort, which includes a casino, on their reservation. "The tribe was originally settled in the Columbia River area, Cascade Mountains and other parts of Oregon, but under the Treaty of 1885, the tribal people relinquished their land but reserved the Warm Springs Reservation for their exclusive use" ("History and Culture."). Now, the Tribe is having a drive to move their casino, Kah-Nee-Ta on the Warm Spring reservation, to their aboriginal land, the Columbia River Gorge area, because the location closer to the Portland area will bring more profit than the existing casino. Congressman David Wu says, "Allowing this proposal will be a bad precedent for Oregon's Indian tribes because breaking Oregon's policy about the Indian casinos will inevitably lead to more off-reservation casinos throughout Oregon" (Wu). Therefore, to prevent more casinos near the Portland area, a new casino should not be constructed in the Columbia Gorge.

Second, a proposed casino will adversely affect the Gorge's environment: "It is estimated that approximately three million people and one million vehicles would visit the proposed casino every year, which will cause an increase in air pollution, traffic and traffic congestion on highways" (Lang). The US Forest Service, in the recently released *Fog and Water Deposition Study,* states that "Acid rain and fog levels within the National Scenic Area are ten to thirty times more acidic than normal rainfall" (qtd. in Wu). Thus, introducing a myriad cars and visitors into the Columbia River Gorge will aggravate these current problems. In addition, the proposed casino will significantly increase the noise, light and water pollution in the Columbia River Gorge. Various kinds of plants and animals inhabit the Columbia River Gorge, including over 800 species of wildflowers, 16 of which exist only in the Columbia River Gorge ("Columbia Gorge"). As a result, the development of the casino would be harmful for the Gorge's wildlife habitats, including existing bald eagle sites, osprey nests, blue heron rookeries, and salmon (Lang).

In addition to the environmental effect, the proposed casino will spoil the scenic beauty of the Gorge. It would be seen from important viewpoints within the National Scenic Area: "the Pacific Crest National Scenic Trail, the Historic Columbia River Highway, Interstate 84 and the Columbia River" (Lang). Also, I often visit the Gorge with my children for hiking and other recreational purposes. Those times, I have seen many families with their children; therefore, if the casino is seen from the Gorge, it will obviously be harmful for children's education. As well as during the day, it would be visible at night because the light system from the huge casino would be illuminated to attract more visitors. Thus, the casino and the beautiful scenery will not be in harmony.

In addition, the casino in the Gorge will make more people addicted to gambling than there are now. The proposed casino will only be forty miles from Portland. Spirit Mountain Casino, currently the biggest and the most lucrative casino in Oregon, is 62 miles from Portland, so if the casino is built in the Gorge, people who don't go to casinos due to the inconvenience of the location of Spirit Mountain Casino would easily be able to access the Gorge casino, and then some of them will be addicted to gambling. Gambling addiction causes severe problems such as abuse, domestic violence, divorce and family breakup. Also, there is a risk that some addicted people would eventually become bankrupt and might steal money to spend on stakes at casinos. In one incident, "A woman, the former West Linn finance director, stole $1.4 million from the city to support a gambling habit and life style from 2000 to 2005, and then she was sentenced to 8 years in prison" (Lednicer). In a 2001 study, "59,000 addictive gamblers were estimated in Oregon and they lost $360 million. Of those beginning treatment, a third had committed illegal acts to support their addiction" (qtd. in Mapes). Therefore, gambling is an addiction as serious as drug addiction. In addition, many people visit the Columbia Gorge for recreational purposes; some of them would turn to the casino after visiting the Gorge. These people may also become addicted to gambling. To prevent more people from being addicted to gambling, the proposed casino should not be allowed.

Lastly, if the casino is built in the Gorge, many small businesses will be affected. People will spend their money on gambling in the casino instead of eating at the restaurants or shopping. The business owners will have to compete with the casino to attract customers and might have to decrease prices to survive against the casino. As their profits are reduced, some of them will inevitably close their businesses, which will be harmful for the local economy and lead to a decrease in the state's revenue.

On the other hand, regardless of the proposed casino's drawbacks, some people say that building a casino will increase the state's revenue and provide better educational opportunity to Oregon children. Since Oregon does not collect a sales tax, state revenue is relatively meager. Thus, the state does not spend enough money on education. Actually, the Portland Public Schools have closed several schools every year due to the lack of funds. Also, Oregon Governor Ted Kulongoski has pledged that "a casino will provide hundreds of millions of dollars to support low-income Oregonians to go to college" ("Opportunity Knocks"). However, casinos and gambling are detrimental for children and education. It is a contradiction that a casino is advantageous for education and children, and it will send the wrong message to students. If our state's leaders are really concerned about education, they should seek other approaches rather than building a casino.

Secondly, it is said that the casino will bring an economic boost to Warm Springs and Cascade Locks. "Over the past eight years, Warm Springs' timber revenue, the tribe's main revenue, has dropped 74%, which resulted in a 33% decline in total revenues. Also, the Tribe is struggling with the problems of a 50% unemployment rate and decreasing job positions" (Suppah). Not only the Warm Springs' economy, but Cascade Locks' economy has also stagnated. There were 90 businesses in the 1950s, but now there are about 19 businesses in the Cascade Locks Industrial Park (Johnson). The tribe has proposed relocating the casino in this almost vacant Cascade Locks Industrial Park. Therefore, the new casino will bring more job opportunities and economic rehabilitation to Warm Springs and Cascade Locks. However, building a new casino needs a significant budget, which will be weighed down with debt because of the tribe's poor financial condition. Even if the new casino makes a large profit, most of the profit will go to investors and the Tribe will not be able to raise as much money as they expect. Instead of building a new casino in the Gorge, the Tribe should expand the current casino and try to attract more tourists to visit Warm Springs.

In addition, proponents claim a new casino will draw more visitors to the Gorge. The proposed casino will provide many facilities for relaxation and entertainment such as hotel, spa, museum, conference center, retail shops and fitness center as well as a casino ("Project Description"). Thus, people will visit the casino to relax and take a break, not specifically just to gamble, because of the convenient location. Now, to relax at a resort, people living in the Portland area go to the Oregon Coast or Central Oregon after driving for two or three hours because there is no such a resort in the Portland area. However, even though the casino would provide resort facilities, it is not a good place to relax with children. Certainly, some people who might visit to use resort facilities would be lured into gambling.

In conclusion, if the casino is built in the Gorge, it will set a precedent to bring more casinos near the Portland area, which would cause many problems. A new casino would harm the Gorge's environment, impair the beautiful scenery, create more gambling addictions, and possibly produce huge debts for the Tribe. Even though the proposed casino would increase the state's revenue and might restore the stagnating economy of Warm Springs and Cascade Locks, the casino should not be built in the Gorge because the drawbacks far outweigh the advantages. If the Tribe wishes to increase their revenue, they should find other approaches: expanding and remodeling their existing casino, or relocating to another site on their reservation. The Columbia River Gorge is an area of rare natural beauty that should be protected from large developments. Itattracts many tourists because of the beautiful scenery and unique ecosystems. Therefore, the Gorge should not be damaged because of a casino or for any other reason.

Works Cited

"Columbia Gorge Overview." *Friends of the Columbia Gorge.* 19 Nov. 2006

    &lt;http://www.gorgefriends.org/gorge.htm&gt;.

"History & Culture." *Warm Springs.* 20 Nov. 2006 &lt;http://www.warmsprings.com/

    Warsprings/Tribal-Community/History-Culture.htmi&gt;.

Johnson, Jean. "State of Oregon Agrees to Off-Reservation Casino." *Indian Country Today*

    19 Apr. 2005. *MasterFile Premier.* EbscoHost. Portland Community College

    Library, Portland, OR. 7 Nov. 2006.

Lang, Michael. United States Congress: Senate. *Oversight Hearing on Indian Gaming.*

    Washington: GPO, 2006.

Lednicer, Lisa Grace. "Embezzler's Sentence: 8 Years." *The Oregonian* 18 Nov. 2006: A01.

    NewsBank. Portland Community College Library, Portland, OR. 20 Nov. 2006.

Mapes, Jeff. "Gambling in Gorge: From Bingo to Billion." *The Oregonian* 22 Dec. 2004: A01.

    NewsBank. Portland Community College Library, Portland, OR. 20 Nov. 2006.

"Opportunity Knocks in the Gorge." Editorial. *The Oregonian* 9 Apr. 2005: C04.

    NewsBank. Portland Community College Library, Portland, OR. 20 Nov. 2006.

"Project Description." *Cascade Locks Resort & Casino Environmental Impact Statement.*

    20 Nov. 2006 &lt;http://www. gorgecasinoeis. corn/project-description.html&gt;.

Suppah, Ron. "Indian Gaming." *FDCH Congressional Testimony* 28 Feb. 2006. *MasterFile

    Premier.* EbscoHost. Portland Community College Library, Portland, OR. 21 Nov.

    2006.

Wu, David. United States Congress: House. *With the Future of the Gorge At Stake. Wu

    Continues His Fight.* 20 Sept. 2005. 7 Nov. 2006 &lt;http://www.house.gov/

    list/press/or01wu/pr09202005gorge.html.